Anonymus

Board of Superintendence of Dublin Hospitals

Forty-First Report with Appendices

Anonymus

Board of Superintendence of Dublin Hospitals
Forty-First Report with Appendices

ISBN/EAN: 9783741197260

Manufactured in Europe, USA, Canada, Australia, Japa

Cover: Foto ©Thomas Meinert / pixelio.de

Manufactured and distributed by brebook publishing software
(www.brebook.com)

Anonymus

Board of Superintendence of Dublin Hospitals

FORTY-FIRST REPORT

OF THE

BOARD OF SUPERINTENDENCE

OF

DUBLIN HOSPITALS,

WITH APPENDICES.

Presented to Parliament by Command of Her Majesty.

DUBLIN:

PRINTED FOR HER MAJESTY'S STATIONERY OFFICE,
BY ALEXANDER THOM & Co. (LIMITED), ABBEY-STREET.

And to be purchased, either directly or through any Bookseller, from
HODGES, FIGGIS, & Co. (LIMITED), 104, GRAFTON-STREET, DUBLIN; or
EYRE & SPOTTISWOODE, EAST HARDING-STREET, FLEET-STREET, E.C., and
32, ABINGDON-STREET, WESTMINSTER, S.W.; or
JOHN MENZIES & Co., 12, HANOVER-STREET, EDINBURGH, and
90, WEST NILE-STREET, GLASGOW.

1899.

CONTENTS.

FORTY-FIRST ANNUAL REPORT

OF THE

BOARD OF SUPERINTENDENCE OF THE DUBLIN HOSPITALS.

TO HIS EXCELLENCY THE RIGHT HON. GEORGE
HENRY, EARL CADOGAN, K.G.,

Lord Lieutenant-General and General Governor of Ireland.

35, Dawson-street,
10th June, 1899.

MAY IT PLEASE YOUR EXCELLENCY:

We have the honour to lay before you the Forty-first Annual
Report on the condition and management of the Dublin Hospitals
which receive Parliamentary grants, and which were duly
inspected by us during the year ending 31st March, 1899.

These are —

1. Westmorland Lock Hospital.
2. The House of Industry Hospitals, viz. :—
   a. Hardwicke Fever Hospital.
   b. Whitworth Medical Hospital.
   a. Richmond Surgical Hospital.

3. Steevens's Hospital.
4. Meath Hospital and County Dublin Infirmary.
5. Cork-street Fever Hospital.
6. Rotunda Lying-in Hospital.
7. Coombe Lying-in Hospital.
8. The Royal Victoria Eye and Ear Hospital; and
9. Royal Hospital for Incurables, which receives a portion
   of the Conondalum Fund.

On making these inspections, we carefully inquired as to the
state and condition of each Institution. We endeavoured to
ascertain if the general management was satisfactory and if due
provision was made for the comforts of the patients, and if the
food was prepared in a careful and economical manner and
presented in a palatable form.

We have seen every patient in the Hospitals and have
interrogated those who appeared most helpless to ascertain if
proper care was bestowed on them.

A 2

We inquired into the nursing arrangements, and to the available means in each Hospital for the extinction of an outbreak of fire, and such other matters as are essential to the welfare and safety of the inmates, in order to report thereon in detail in accordance with Act 19 and 20 Vic., cap. 110.

With the object of more effectively dealing with the cure and the prevention of disease, we were pleased to find that bacteriological investigations are, at the present time, earnestly engaging the attention of the Medical Authorities.

As previously stated in a former Report, most of these Hospitals admit applicants without any recommendation, and merely from being considered on examination by the Medical attendants to be fit objects for treatment. With regard, however, to the admission of certain cases of pulmonary phthisis into general wards, we are of opinion that in the interest of other patients, and of the community at large, it would be desirable for the Local Government Board to provide special sanatoria in suitable localities for the separate treatment of such patients. If this scheme could be carried out it would greatly relieve the pressure on the City Hospitals, and the expenditure involved would in the end prove an economy, and prevent the spread of tuberculous diseases.

We venture also to suggest that the public should be informed by the authorities of the ways in which tuberculous diseases may be disseminated, and the means by which they may be obviated.

We cannot forbear adding that it would be advisable that strict sanitary legislation should be enforced in regard to public conveyances, and also to churches, school-rooms, theatres, factories, markets, and dairy-yards, and other buildings where large assemblies of people are gathered together.

The various Statistical and other Tables in Appendices will be found similar in character to those that have hitherto appeared in regular annual sequence, but at the same time indicative of the relative changes and results in the operation of the different institutions.

The financial accounts are rendered on a **uniform system**, so that it can be seen whether any Hospital is **extravagant in its** expenditure as compared with others.

The figures generally afford a satisfactory proof that the governing bodies are showing a due regard to economy in the arrangements for the maintenance of patients in the several Hospitals under their management.

From the records and vouchers that have come under our notice, it is evident that great care is taken in the making of contracts, and that the goods supplied are scrutinized, so as to ensure that they are equal to standard and not deficient in quantity.

On the 1st of April, 1899, there remained 992 patients in these Hospitals under the supervision of our Board.

The number admitted during the year was 11,492, making the whole number under treatment 12,484, of whom 10,991 left the wards either cured or relieved, or were discharged for other causes, and 498 died.

Nine hundred and ninety-five remained under treatment in these Hospitals on the 31st March, 1899.

Exclusive of incurables, the mortality was 4·1 per cent. on those treated to a termination.

The total daily average number of beds occupied in these Hospitals throughout the year was 952·63.

The time spent in Hospital by each patient under treatment (omitting the patients in the Royal Hospital for Incurables) averaged 23·43 days.

Appendix.—Table No. 1 shows a list of diseases of patients treated in the several Hospitals and the number that died of any particular disease during the year ended 31st March, 1899.

Table No. 2 shows the average cost per bed occupied throughout the year ending 31st March, 1899, for maintenance and for establishment, and for both, exclusive of buildings and furniture.

Table No. 3 shows the several sources of income of each Hospital.

Table No. 4 sets forth in detail the chief heads of expenditure of each Hospital.

Table No. 5 gives the number of patients treated in each Hospital, the mortality per cent., the average daily number of beds occupied during the year, and the present extent of accommodation for each class of patients.

Table No. 6 shows the prices of articles supplied to each Hospital per contract or otherwise.

Table No. 7 gives the various dietaries in use in each Hospital.

Table No. 8 gives the names of the Governors of each Hospital, and number of attendances during the year.

We wish to call the attention of the wealthy inhabitants of Dublin to the many needed improvements in these Hospitals, which are worthy of attention and assistance; but as in many cases available funds are insufficient for effecting these advances, we hope that such help may be afforded as may enable these Institutions to keep out of debt, and to carry out their beneficent work to the advantage of the whole community.

WESTMORLAND LOCK HOSPITAL.

We have not much to notice in this Hospital as having been effected in the way of alteration or improvements since our last Inspection. We found it in a satisfactory condition as regards the comforts of the patients, and no complaint was made to us during our visit as to the want of attention on the part of attendants.

The cooking, and the distribution of the diets are conducted according to regulation. The quality of the food is good, and the returns and vouchers in connection with expenditure are accurately kept.

The beds and bed-clothes were clean and in order, and white quilts were in use, by which arrangement soiling is at once observed and the want of a change immediately indicated.

We regret to have observed in one ward, a press containing soiled linen. This arrangement is objectionable, and we hope some better provision may be made to remedy this insanitary condition. We have frequently pointed out in previous Reports that soiled linen should not be kept in wards or allowed to accumulate in lobbies, bath-rooms or closets attached to the wards.

The senior Surgeon to this Hospital, who is himself a member of this Board, states:—

(a) "That the clothes supplied to the patients as being insufficiently warm for patients under specific treatment, and that the uniform which they are required to wear partakes too much of the character of prison clothes; it is therefore distasteful to the patients, and tends to prevent them from availing themselves of the benefit of the hospital in the early stages of venereal disease.

(b) The appliances for the examination and treatment of the patients are old-fashioned and behind the time.

(c) Antiseptic treatment, which is essential in order effectually to deal with venereal diseases, is impossible at present in the Hospital, owing to the want of the necessary appliances to enable the surgeons to carry it out.

(d) The nurses, although respectable, painstaking women, have received no regular training and are uncertified, with the exception of the Maternity Nurse, who holds a midwifery diploma. This state of things militates against the efficiency of the Hospital in checking venereal diseases. It deters patients from seeking early admission, and tends to make them seek treatment outside the Hospital. The Board of Governors plead insufficiency of funds as their reason for not being able to remedy these defects."

The Matron discharges her duties with much zeal, and continues to exercise a judicious avoidance of irksome discipline in the management of the inmates.

There were 54 patients in this institution on the 1st April, 1898; 417 were admitted, and 11 infants were born in the house during the year; 396 were discharged; 14 died; and 72 remained on the 31st March, 1899.

The mortality was 3·4 per cent. on the total number treated to a termination.

The time spent in Hospital by each patient averaged 50 days, and the average daily number of beds occupied during the year was 66·67.

STEEVENS'S HOSPITAL.

We have pleasure in stating that this Hospital continues to be maintained in a state of efficiency which is creditable to all concerned.

We have in the course of our inspection gone over the whole building, and found the wards and corridors in a very satisfactory condition. The rations were of good quality, and the kitchen accommodation and cooking utensils sufficient and in order.

We examined the surgical appliances and the instruments under the care of the Resident Surgeon, and found them in good order and well arranged. We were informed that at all times careful precautions are taken for immediate treatment of cases of poisoning. We recommend, however, that a toxicological chart be hung up in a conspicuous place, which would show at a glance the antidotes and appropriate measures indicated in such cases. For, notwithstanding a careful toxicological training, a medical officer, in the hurry of an emergency, might find his memory fail him. The Resident Surgeon discharges his professional duties with conscientiousness, and with much ability; but we are of opinion that it is worthy of consideration whether it would not be advisable to appoint in addition a junior house surgeon, so that in the absence of one qualified medical officer the other should remain on duty in the Hospital.

Within the last few years the Governors found it necessary to remodel the whole sanitary arrangements, and among other recent improvements the following may be noted:—

The operating theatre has been completely reconstructed upon the most modern principles, so as to secure complete asepsis in operating, and two wards have been annexed to it for the reception of patients after serious operations; this has entailed an outlay of nearly £2,000.

A large destructor or crematorium has been erected, in which contaminated articles of dressings are destroyed.

A pathological laboratory has been established, and also a complete apparatus for taking skiograms by the Röntgen process, now so largely used for the detection of fractures and foreign bodies.

A new laundry, fitted with the most modern and complete equipment, has recently replaced the old and defective one. In connection with this department, we have ascertained that the clothes are as much as possible dried and aired in the open air, and that articles used by patients affected by contagious diseases are steeped, boiled, and washed separately.

The increasing demand for trained nurses had rendered it obligatory on the Governors to greatly extend the nursing staff, and as suitable accommodation could not be obtained for nurses and probationers in the main building without still further encroachments on the wards intended for the use of the sick poor, a new Nurses' Home is now in course of erection, and has nearly reached its completion. This, however, has entailed a cost of more than £9,500, of which a very large balance must still be made up.

The new Home is intended to accommodate fifty nurses and probationers, separate quarters being provided for those attending infectious diseases.

On the 1st April, 1898, 104 patients remained in Hospital; 1,352 were admitted during the year; 1,298 were discharged; 38 died; and 120 remained at the close of the year.

The mortality was 2·8 per cent. on the total treated to a termination.

The time spent in Hospital by each patient averaged 26·27 days, and the average daily number of beds occupied during the year was 104·79.

THE MEATH HOSPITAL.

The result of our inspection of this Hospital was to confirm the opinion expressed in previous Reports as to the energetic and progressive spirit in which it is managed. The medical and surgical work of the Hospital has always been of a high order, and the records of cases show the care and attention bestowed on the patients; the nurses under the Lady Superintendent, we have been informed, are kind, capable, and assiduous in discharging their duties. During the past year every department has been maintained in an efficient state. The kitchen and cooking arrangements have been carefully attended to. The provisions are of the best quality.

The permanent improvements which we alluded to in our last year's Report as being in progress are now completed, and have left nothing to be desired in point of efficiency.

These consist of :—

(1.) A new male accident ward, containing 12 beds, fitted with separate bathroom, lavatory, &c. The ward is lofty and admirably ventilated and lighted, and suitably furnished.

(2.) A new operating theatre, which is in every respect up-to-date, and fitted with all modern requirements.

(3.) The laundry has been remodelled and enlarged, and provided with all necessary machinery, &c.

(4.) A new steam boiler has been erected, which supplies steam and hot water to the laundry, heats the theatre, and sterilizes the water used in operations. A new hot water circulating system for supplying the baths, &c., throughout the Hospital has been provided, which also is heated from this new steam boiler.

We find the sum of £3,589 has already been paid on account of these improvements, leaving a balance still due of about £300.

We were pleased to be informed that, since the first announcement of the discovery of the X Rays, the Röntgen Ray Skiographic investigation has been carried out at this Hospital, and has contributed much to the alleviation of suffering and to the more accurate diagnosis of many of the more obscure forms of disease and injury.

There were 111 patients in this Hospital at the commencement of the year; 1,143 were admitted; 1,077 discharged; 70 died; and 112 remained on the 31st March, 1899.

The mortality was 6·1 per cent. on the total number treated to a termination.

The time spent in Hospital by each patient averaged 27 days, and the average daily number of beds occupied during the year was 93·12.

CORK STREET FEVER HOSPITAL.

The inspection of this Hospital enables us to give a favourable report of its general condition. We found every department maintained in an efficient state, and that order and neatness pervaded all arrangements throughout.

We found the patients suitably provided for, and every effort appears to be made to render them as comfortable as possible.

We ascertained that provision exists for the isolation of certain forms of infectious fever, and that there is a separate detached apartment where discharged patients are bathed and receive their own clothing thoroughly disinfected previous to returning home.

The drainage of the Hospital and of the Beneavin Home has been inspected by the Dublin Sanitary Association, and found in perfect order. Alterations have been made in the plumbing arrangements of the Red House, and the passages and the wards have been recently painted, which adds much to the appearance of the Hospital.

We have been informed that the Managing Committee have approached the landlord of dairy yards adjoining the Hospital with a view to purchase the premises, which will afford ample space to build a suitable house for the nursing staff, and which will enable the Managing Committee to erect a ring fence round the institution.

Towards the latter end of the financial year, the number of patients having diminished, the Committee were enabled to send out to Unions and private houses a few of their disengaged nurses. Application had often been made previously to supply nurses to the public, but their services were so much required in the Hospital that it was found not possible to spare one.

The Hospital supplies were of good quality, and the returns and vouchers in connection with their expenditure accurately kept.

We consider the Matron is deserving of much praise for the neat and systematic arrangement of the store-room.

If funds were available we suggest as an improvement the replacement of the present baths in use by the porcelain ware pattern, which is specially adapted to ensure cleanliness and would obviate the necessity of frequent painting.

At the commencement of the year 187 remained in the Hospital; 2,028 were admitted; 1,803 were discharged; 106 died; and 151 remained on the 31st March, 1890.

The mortality was 8·00 per cent. on those treated to a termination.

The average daily number of beds* occupied, including Beneavin Convalescent Home was 164·91, and the time spent in Hospital by each patient averaged 27·4 days.

HOUSE OF INDUSTRY HOSPITALS.

It is evident that great energy and earnestness is shown in the general management and administration of this Institution, and valuable opportunities are afforded by each Hospital for promoting medical education.

We found the wards clean and in order, and the various articles of food, including bread, meat, beef tea, and milk, &c., without exception, of good quality.

The assiduous attention of the Lady Superintendent to the requirements of the patients and the devotion of the nursing staff to their duties, leaves nothing to report but what is satisfactory.

We examined the medical and surgical records, which are carefully kept, and which show in the most satisfactory manner the care and attention which is bestowed on every detail of treatment by a medical staff of distinguished ability.   We are of opinion that, as a matter of discipline and for scientific requirement, a regular, systematic, and thorough habit of case-taking should be insisted on in all Hospitals.

We have ascertained that great care is taken that everything should be in readiness for any emergency in case of poisoning, and that the various appliances and antidotes are kept ready for immediate use.

We found the general stores arranged with order and neatness under the care of the Sister in charge, and that strict economy is constantly kept in view, and that nothing is permitted to be lost or wasted.

We are unable to report as fully as we could wish on the new erection which is to replace the Richmond Hospital; but considerable progress has been made with the building, and it is expected to be in occupation next year. So far as we can at present judge it will not be surpassed by any similar Hospital in the United Kingdom in respect to completeness and efficiency.

We were informed that pathological research is as far as possible carried out, and that a fair amount of microscopical work is done, but we hope that better arrangements may be made for the prosecution of bacteriological research, now so essential in Hospitals, and for which we doubt not the Governors will provide the necessary room and appliances.

We are glad to be able to report that many of our former suggestions have been adopted and carried into effect; those not as yet acted on, will, we feel sure, receive due consideration at the hands of the Governors.

WHITWORTH MEDICAL HOSPITAL.

On the 1st April, 1898, 47 patients remained in Hospital, 704 were admitted; 661 were discharged; 40 died; giving a mortality of 0·50 per cent, on the total number of cases treated to a termination.

The average daily number of beds occupied was 38·08; and the time spent in Hospital by each patient under treatment averaged 18·08 days.

RICHMOND SURGICAL HOSPITAL.

There were 59 patients in this Hospital when the year commenced; 820 were admitted; 789 were discharged; 39 died; giving a mortality of 4·71 per cent. on the total number of cases treated to a termination.

The average daily number of beds occupied in the year was 55·60; and the time spent in Hospital by each patient averaged 20·47 days.

ROTUNDA LYING-IN HOSPITAL.

We were much gratified by the order, regularity, and cleanliness which prevailed, and by the kindness and attention bestowed on the patients.

The wards were bright and well ventilated, and the beds and bedclothes were properly attended to.

We ascertained that the soiled linen is promptly removed from the wards, tied up in bundles, and placed in the foul linen shaft, and from thence is daily carried to the laundry. The washed clothes are returned from the laundry in baskets, and conveyed to each storey by a special lift without coming in contact with the contaminated articles.

We are of opinion that some improvement might be made for the better ventilation of this shaft, and that it would be advisable to have it periodically disinfected. Other parts of the buildings appeared in good order, and the drainage is said to be efficient.

We were particularly pleased with the gynæcological department, in which a large number of cases are treated annually. This building consists of three stories, each of which is connected by corridors with the corresponding level of the Lying-in-Hospital. It contains five well-ventilated wards, having sixteen beds each, and three smaller wards for special cases. The bathrooms and lavatories are of the most approved description.

The operating theatre is equipped with the most modern appliances, and seems admirably suited to the objects for which it has been designed.

Many minor matters in the way of renovation and decoration are under the consideration of the Governors, and we have no doubt that these improvements will soon be carried out.

As a school for giving instruction in Midwifery and for the diseases peculiar to women it holds the highest reputation, and the renown of its clinical teaching continues to attract a large number of students from all parts of the world.

On the 1st of April, 1898, there were 40 patients in the labour wards; 1,780 were admitted during the year; 281 were discharged not having been delivered; 5 died; and 40 remained in the Hospital at the end of the year.

Thirty-three patients remained in the auxiliary or chronic department on the 1st of April, 1898; 559 were admitted; 548 discharged; 14 died in the year ended 31st March, 1890, and 30 then remained.

The average daily number of beds occupied throughout the year by labour cases was 40·87, and that of the chronic class was 20·05.

The time spent in Hospital by labour cases averaged 8·1 days, and that by the chronic class 18·47 days.

The mortality in the labour wards, deducting non-parturient cases, was 0·33 per cent., and that of the chronic class 2·4 per cent.

COOMBE LYING-IN HOSPITAL.

The state of the wards and the condition of the patients were satisfactory in view of the difficulty of the management which arises out of the limited resources of the hospital. It merits a liberal support, not only on account of the benefit it confers on the poor, but also on the advantages it affords in forwarding medical education. As the district in which it is situated is very poor and densely populated, we were glad to be informed that a comprehensive scheme has recently been initiated by Lord Ardilaun, Lord Iveagh, and Mr. James Talbot Power, who have obtained an Act of Parliament to convert an insanitary area in the vicinity of the Hospital into a public garden. This undertaking will prove beneficial to a large number of extern labour cases who are annually attended in this neighbourhood by students from the Hospital.

It is the intention of the Guardians and Directors to provide additional accommodation for nurses, which will enable a larger number to be trained in the Hospital.

We believe that this special branch of nursing is much required throughout the country, and it is probable that it will assume additional importance owing to the fact that many appointments are likely to be made under the Local Government Board new regulations.

We consider there is much need for a hot air chamber or a fumigating apparatus for disinfecting patients' clothes previous to being stowed away. We have no doubt this matter will receive due attention from the Guardians and Directors.

We were informed that the supply of linen is now ample, a matter of great importance, as it permits the clothes to be retained sufficiently long at the laundry for thorough washing and purification.

On the 1st April, 1898, there were 17 patients in the labour wards; 009 were admitted during the year; 155 were discharged, not having been delivered; 2 died; and 21 remained in the Hospital at the close of the year.

Nine patients remained in the chronic wards on the 1st of April, 1898; 207 were admitted; 201 were discharged; 3 died; 12 remained at the end of the year.

The average daily number of beds occupied throughout the year by labour cases was 1978 and that by chronic cases 14·00.

The time spent in Hospital by labour patients averaged 8·03 days, and that by the chronic class 23·8 days.

The mortality of patients admitted to the chronic wards was 1.47 on those treated to a termination, and that of the labour class was 0·4 per cent.

THE ROYAL VICTORIA EYE AND EAR HOSPITAL.

We visited St. Mark's and the National Eye and Ear Infirmary, which have recently been amalgamated, and now constitute the "Royal Victoria Eye and Ear Hospital." This institution is doing a good deal of useful work, so far as structural defects admit; the Council are, however, anxious to procure a suitable site for the erection of a new Hospital, the plans of which we are confident will be carefully and judiciously considered, so that every detail may be arranged after the most modern methods, and with a view to economy in its management. The success of this undertaking will depend on the liberality of the public, and we hope that the founders may soon be able to extend the charitable objects for which it is intended. There can be no doubt that it will prove highly valuable as a means of enabling students to acquire a more extended knowledge of the diseases of the eye and ear, and also of alleviating the sufferings endured by the poor.

The records of cases are kept with care, which must be of great advantage for future reference.

We regret that a serious accident should have occurred in the Molesworth-street branch of this Institution in November last, as a result of which a patient died. It appears that an old man who had been successfully operated on for cataract, opened a window on the first floor during the night (while suffering from mental derangement), got out through it, and fell to the ground, sustaining a fracture of the leg. The best surgical aid was obtained for him, but the unfortunate man died of pneumonia a week afterwards.

We hope that means may be taken to prevent the recurrence of such an accident, and consider that a nurse should be constantly on duty at night time.

On the 1st of April, 1898, 00 patients were in Hospital; 1,118 were admitted during the year; 1,116 were discharged; and 61 then remained.

The average daily number of beds occupied during the year was 69, and the time spent in Hospital by each patient averaged 21·4 days.

One death occurred in the Hospital during the year.

THE ROYAL HOSPITAL FOR INCURABLES.

We found this Hospital in all its arrangements and equipments in admirable order and efficiency.

The medical care and treatment of the patients was very satisfactory, and much liberality is shown in the efforts to promote as far as possible their general comfort and well-being.

The Governors are entitled to great credit for the energy they have evinced in the maintenance and management of this useful and charitable institution.

The large wards devoted specially to cases of consumption and cancer merit our highest approval, these class of cases being those which engage the principal attention of the medical and surgical staff of this most important Hospital.

Two hundred and sixteen patients remained in Hospital on the 1st of April, 1898; 60 were admitted; 0 were discharged, resigned or went out on pension; 47 died during the year; and 216 remained on the 31st March, 1899.

The time spent in Hospital by each patient averaged 281·03 days.

The average daily number of beds occupied throughout the year was 210·1.

We have the honour to be

Your Excellency's obedient, faithful servants,

POWERSCOURT, *Chairman.*
FRANCIS W. BRADY, Bart.
ARDILAUN.
JOHN E. BARRY, Knt.
JOSEPH WOODLOCK.
PERCY R. GRACE, Bart.
JOHN BANKS, K.C.B.
LAMBERT H. ORMSBY, M.D.
CHARLES K. LAMBKIN.
THOMAS A. DICKSON, P.C.
HENRY FITZGIBBON, M.D.
JOHN MAGEE FINNY, M.D.

WILLIAM J. MARTIN, *Secretary.*

APPENDIX.

TABLE No. 1.

A CLASSIFIED RETURN of the DISEASES of Patients treated in the HARDWICKE FEVER, WHITWORTH MEDICAL, and RICHMOND SURGICAL HOSPITALS; of the number of such Patients affected with, and of the number that died of, any particular Disease during the Year ended 31st March, 1899.

HOUSE OF INDUSTRY GOVERNMENT HOSPITALS.

THE HARDWICKE FEVER HOSPITAL.

Disease.	No. Treated.	No. Died.	Disease.	No. Treated.	No. Died.
Abscess, Glandular,	1	—	Herpes,	1	—
„ Peri-Typhylitis,	1	—			
Alcoholism,	1	1			
Ague,	1	—	Intestinal Obstruction,	2	—
Anæmia,	2	—	Influenza,	6	—
Ascites,	1	1			
Bronchitis,	10	3	Laryngitis,	1	—
Broncho-Pneumonia,	5	3	Laryngysmus Stridulus,	1	—
Cancrum Oris,	1	1	Meningitis,	8	7
Cellulitis,	3	1	Microcephalic,	1	—
Constipation,	6	—			
Convulsions,	1	—			
Croup,	2	—	Parotitis,	6	—
			Pericarditis,	1	1
			Peritonitis,	1	—
Dementia,	1	—	Pertussis,	1	—
Diabetes,	1	1	Phthisis, Pulmonalis,	3	—
Diarrhœa,	3	—	Pleuritis,	1	1
Diphtheria,	45	7	Pneumonia,	23	3
Endocarditis,	1	—			
			Rheumatism, Acute,	8	—
Erysipelas,	42	—			
Erythema,	1	—	Scarlatina,	148	8
			Syphilis,	2	—
Fever, Febricula,	22	—			
„ Enteric,	280	16	Tonsillitis,	19	—
„ Typhus,	8	1	Ulcerative Stomatitis,	1	—
Gangrene,	1	—	Urticaria,	3	—
Gastritis,	4	—			
Gonorrhœa,	1	—	Varicella,	6	—

WHITWORTH MEDICAL HOSPITAL.

Disease.	No. Treated.	No. Died.	Disease.	No. Treated.	No. Died.
Abscess,	9	1	Hydrocele,	10	—
Addison's,	2	1	Hydro-Pneumic Thorax,	1	—
Ague,	3	—	Hyperchondriasis,	2	—
Alopecia,	1	—	Hysteria,	6	—
Alcoholism,	10	1	Impetigo,	2	—
Amyloid Kidneys,	1	—	Inflammation Alveolar,	1	—
Anæmia,	29	—	Influenza,	13	—
Aneurism,	7	1	Jaundice,	4	—
Angina Pectoris,	3	—	Laryngitis,	3	1
Anæmic,	7	1	Locomotor Ataxy,	6	—
Arthritis,	2	—	Lumbago,	3	—
Asthenia,	2	—	Malaria,	1	—
Asthma,	3	—	Meningitis,	3	3
Atrophy,	3	—	Masturbation,	1	—
Atheroma,	3	—	Melancholia,	1	—
Bright's,	11	1	Mitral Regurgitation,	12	3
Bronchitis,	36	2	Nephritis,	10	1
" Chronic,			Neuralgia,	2	—
Broncho-Pneumonia,	2	1	Neurasthenia,	1	1
Calculus,	2	—	Neuritis,	7	1
Cancer,	4	—	Obstruction, Fœcal,	5	1
Cardiac,	26	5	Pains, Abdominal,	1	—
Chlorosis,	3	—	Paralysis,	3	1
Chorea,	16	—	" Agitans,	3	—
Cirrhosis of Liver,	23	5	Paraplegia,	6	1
Colitis,	1	—	Pemphigus,	1	1
Congenital Want of De-			Pericarditis,	1	—
velopment,	1	—	Perisplenitis,	1	—
Constipation,	10	1	Peritonitis,	1	1
Convulsions,	1	—	Petit Mal,	4	—
Coryza,	1	—	Phlebitis,	11	—
Cystitis,	1	—	Phthisis, Pulmonalis,	45	1
Debility,	2	—	Plural Effusion,	11	1
Delirium Tremens,	1	—	Pleuritis,	11	1
Dermatitis,	7	—	Pleurisy,	9	—
Diabetes,	1	—	Plumbism,	2	—
Diarrhœa,	8	—	Pleuro pneumonia,	3	—
Diphtheria,	2	—	Pneumonia,	19	2
Dilated Stomach,	4	—	Poisoning,	2	—
Dyspepsia,	16	—	Poliomyelitis,	2	—
Eczema,	7	—	Prurigo,	1	—
Elephantiasis,	2	—	Psoriasis,	6	—
Empyema,	1	—	Rheumatism,	16	—
Emphysema,	5	—	Rheumatic Arthitis,	3	—
Endocarditis,	25	4	sciatica,	3	—
Epilepsy,	4	—	Sclerosis,	3	—
Erysipelas,	3	—	Scarlatina,	1	—
Erythema,	2	—	Sarcoma,	1	—
Fever, Enteric,	44	1	Steatorrhœa Sicca,	1	—
" Rheumatic,	1	—	splenitis,	1	—
" Typhus,	1	—	Spine Disease,	1	—
" Febricula,	2	—	" Injury to,	1	—
Friedrich's,	1	—	Stricture of the Œsophagus,	1	—
Gallstones,	1	—	Syphilis,	8	—
Gastritis,	6	1	Tachycardia,	1	—
Gastro Dynia,	1	—	Tetanus,	1	—
Goitre,	3	—	Torticollis,	2	—
Gonorrhœa,	2	—	Tonsilitis,	3	—
Gout,	6	—	Tumour,	2	—
Hæmoptysis,	3	—	" in Brain,	1	—
Hernia Strangulated,		—	" Abdominal,	1	—
Hemiplegia,	9	1	Ulcers,	7	—
Hepatitis,	1	—	Uterine Fibroid,	1	—
Herpes Zoster,	1	—	" Polypus,	1	—
Hodgkin's,	3	1	Varicella,	1	—

Disease.	No. Treated	No. Died	Disease.	No. Treated	No. Died
Abortion,	1	—	Cystitis,	4	—
Abscess,	33	2	Deformity,	1	—
„ Psoas,	2	—	Deflected Sept. Nasi,	1	—
„ in Knee Joint,	2	2	Dentition,	1	—
„ Temporo-sphenoidal lobe,	9	2	Dyspepsia,	1	—
„ Ischiatic Post Natal,	3	—	Eclampsia,	1	—
Acne, Rosacea,	1	—	Empyema,	1	—
Adenoma,	2	—	Enlarged Tonsils,	3	—
Adenitis,	1	—	Epididymitis,	2	—
Alcoholism,	5	—	Epilepsy,	3	—
Aneurism,	2	—	Epiphysial Separation of Humerus,	3	—
Anthrax,	6	2	Erysipelas,	4	—
Ankylosis,	2	—	Eversion of Lip,	1	—
Appendicitis,	4	—	Exostosis,	2	—
Atony of Bladder,	1	—	Exposure,	1	—
Broncho Pneumonia,	1	—			
Bubo, Suppurative,	4	—	Fever, Typhoid,	2	—
Burns and Scalds,	11	2	Fistula in Ano,	6	—
Bunions,	1	—	„ Perineal,	1	—
Bursitis,	3	—	„ Vesico Vaginal,	2	—
Calculus,	4	1	Foreign Bodies in Knee Joint,	1	—
„ Salivary,	1	—			
Cancer of Bladder,	1	—	Fracture, Compound, of Fingers,	3	—
„ Penis,	1	—	„ Compound, of Leg,	4	1
„ Lip,	10	—	„ Compound, of Elbow,	2	—
„ Cheek,	1	—	„ Cond. of Knee,	1	—
„ Stomach,	5	1	„ of Tibia,	3	—
„ Head,	1	—	„ Femur,	7	1
„ Ear,	1	—	„ Tibia and Fibula,	10	—
„ Uterus,	5	—	„ Clavicle,	3	—
„ Jaw,	5	—	„ Jaw,	1	—
„ Tongue,	7	—	„ Ribs,	11	—
„ Rectum,	6	—	„ Nasal Bones,	1	1
„ Larynx,	2	2	„ Elbow,	1	—
„ Neck,	3	—	„ Skull,	6	1
„ Prostate,	5	—	„ Patella,	4	—
„ Breast,	12	—	„ Humerus,	2	—
„ Nose,	1	—	„ Foot,	1	—
„ Colon,	1	1	„ Malleolus,	1	—
„ Thumb,	1	—			
„ Mouth,	2	—	Gangrene,	4	3
Caseated Gland in Neck,	1	—	Gallstones,	1	—
Carcinoma of Breast,	1	—	Gastritis,	1	—
Cardiac Failure,	1	—	Gingivitis,	1	—
Caries of Spine,	7	1	Goitre,	1	—
„ Femur,	3	—	Gonorrhœa,	4	—
„ Humerus,	1	—	Gumma,	1	—
„ Ribs,	1	—			
Cataract,	1	—	Hæmatemesis,	1	—
Catarrh, Nasal,	1	—	Hæmatoma,	1	—
Cellulitis,	3	—	Hæmaturia,	1	—
Colic,	1	—	Hæmorrhage,	3	—
Concussion of Brain,	3	1	„ Cerebral,	1	—
Contraction of Hand,	1	—	Hæmorrhoids,	3	—
„ Fingers,	2	—	Hare Lip,	1	—
„ Knee,	2	—	Heart, Malignant Disease of,	5	—
Conjunctivitis,	2	—	Hydrocele,	6	—
Constipation,	1	—			
Contusion,	12	—			
Convulsions,	14	2			
Cysts,	8	—			

Appendix
No. 1

Richmond
Surgical
Hospital

Disease.	No. Treated	No. Died	Disease.	No. Treated	No. Died
Hydrocephalus,	1	–	Prolapsus Uteri,	2	–
Hypertrophic Rhinitis,	5	–	Prostate, Enlarged,	3	2
Hypochondriasis,	7	–			
Hernia, Strangulated,	5	–	Rickets,	1	–
,, Inguinal	12	–	Rheumatism, Acute,	1	–
,, Double Scrotal,	2	–	,, Chronic,	2	–
,, Incarcerated,	1	1	Ruptured Ligaments,	1	–
,, Umbilical,	1	–	,, Quadriceps Ten-		
,, Obstructed,	3	–	don,	1	–
Hysteria,	7	–	Scabies,	1	–
Hysterical Torticollis,	1	–	Sciatica,	1	–
			Scirrhus of Breast,	1	–
Immersion,	5	–	Sclerosis,	1	–
Indigestion,	1	–	Sarcoma,	1	–
Injuries,	5	–	Sinus,	7	–
Insanity,	1	–	Spine, Curvature of, and		
Intussusceptio,	2	–	Paraplegia,	1	1
			,, Potts,	1	–
Laryngitis,	2	–	Stricture of the Œsopha-		
Leucocythæmia,	1	–	gus,	3	1
Lipoma,	6	–	,, Urethra,	21	1
Lumbago,	1	–	Starvation,	2	–
Lupus,	1	–	Stenosis Cervix Uteri,	2	–
Luxations,	5	–	Synovitis,	9	–
Lymphadenitis,	2	–	Syphilis,	7	–
Locomotor Ataxy,	1	–	Syphilitic Pharyngitis,	1	–
Malingering,	1	–	Talipes,	10	–
Morbus Coxæ,	14	2	Tonsillitis,	1	–
Mastoid,	2	–	Tumours,	5	–
Meningitis,	1	1	Tubercular Taes Synovitis,	1	–
Mastitis,	1	–	,, Knee,	20	–
Metritis, Endo-	6	–	,, Glands,	17	–
Multiple Melanotic Sarco-			,, Kidneys,	2	1
mata,	1	–	,, Toes,	3	–
			,, Sternum,	2	–
Necrosis,	36	–	,, Ankle,	2	–
Node in Clavicle,	1	–	,, Metatarsus,	3	–
Nephritis,	1	–	,, Hip,	1	–
Neuroma,	2	–	,, Testes,	2	–
			,, Wrist,	2	–
Obstruction of Bowel, Chron-	2	1	,, Peritonitis,	3	–
,, Acute,	6	1	,, Elbow,	3	–
Orchitis,	6	–	,, Foot,	1	–
Osteitis,	1	–	,, Meningitis,	1	–
Otitis, Media,	1	–			
Ovarium,	1	–	Ulcers,	14	–
			,, Rodent,	4	–
Palate, Cleft,	7	–	,, Varicose,	7	–
Paralysis,	9	–	,, Perforating of		
Paraphymosis,	1	–	Stomach,	1	–
Paraplegia,	9	–	Urine, Retention of,	6	–
Paronychia,	1	–	,, Suppression of,	1	–
Paresis,	1	–	Uræmic Coma,	1	1
Periostitis,	1	–			
Peritonitis, Tubercular,	1	1	Varicose Veins,	35	–
,, Suppurative,	1	1	Varicocele,	4	–
Phimosis,	1	–			
Phlebitis,	1	–	Wounds,	26	–
Pleurisy,	1	–	,, Ear torn off,	1	–
Poisoning,	2	–	Whitlow,	3	–
Polypus Uteri,	4	–	Wry,	2	–
Post-Nasal Adenoids,	2	–			

MEATH HOSPITAL, Year ended 31st March, 1899.

Disease.	No. Treated.	No. Died.	Disease.	No. Treated.	No. Died.
Abscess, Acute,	18	—	Delirium Tremens,	1	—
" Chronic,	6	3	Diabetes,	3	—
" Renal,	1	—	Debility,	10	—
Acne,	2	—	Diarrhœa,	4	—
Alcoholism,	7	1	Diphtheria,	4	1
Anæmia,	14	—	Dropsy,	6	1
Aneurism of Aorta,	1	—	Dyspepsia,	11	—
Antrax,	1	1			
Ankylosis of Elbow,	1	—			
" Knee,	3	—			
Anus, Fistula in,	3	—			
Aortic Patency,	4	1	Eczema,	7	—
Apoplexy,	6	—	Emphysema,	3	1
Arthritis,	2	—	Enteritis,	1	—
Ascarides,	2	—	Epilepsy,	4	—
Ascites,	5	—	Epistaxis,	2	—
Asthma,	8	1	Epulis,	2	—
			Erysipelas,	3	—
			Erythema,	2	—
Bronchitis, Acute (Bronchopneumonia),	18	2	Exostosis,	2	—
" Chronic,	14	—			
Bubo,	4	—			
Burns and Scalds,	14	1	Fever, Scarlet,	17	2
Bursitis, Acute,	6	—	" Enteric,	50	2
			" Chicken-pox,	3	—
			" Whooping-cough,	3	—
			" Measles,	6	—
Calculus in Urethra,	7	—	Fistula in Ano,	4	—
" Bladder,	1	—	Fracture of Clavicle,	1	—
Cancer of Breast,	7	—	" Femur,	9	1
" Jaw,	2	—	" Fibula,	16	—
" Lips,	3	—	" Humerus,	3	—
" Intestines,	3	1	" Patella,	5	—
" Liver,	2	—	" Radius,	3	—
" Tongue,	4	—	" Ribs,	5	—
" Thyroid,	1	1	" Skull,	1	—
Carcinoma,	14	2	" Base of,	1	1
Cardiitis,	4	—	" Tibia,	10	—
Caries of Tibia,	2	—	" Tibia & Fibula combined,	9	—
" Hand,	3	—			
" Spine,	1	—			
Catarrh,	16	—			
Chancre,	6	—			
Cheumaia,	1	—	Gangrene of Leg,	1	1
Chlorosis,	13	—	Gastritis,	7	—
Crouitorea,	1	—	Gastro Enteritis,	1	—
Chorea,	6	—	Genu Valgum,	3	—
Choroiditis,	2	—	Gonorrhœa,	8	—
Cirrhosis of Liver,	4	1	Gout,	2	—
" Kidney,	3	—			
Cleft Palate,	1	—			
Colic,	2	—			
Colitis, Phlegmon,	4	—			
Concussion of Brain,	1	1	Hæmatemesis,	8	—
" Spine,	1	—	Hæmoptysis,	3	—
Conjunctivitis,	3	—	Hæmorrhage, Cerebral,	3	1
Constipation,	2	—	Hæmorrhoids,	4	—
Contusion,	6	—	Hare Lip,	1	—
Convulsions,	4	1	Heart, Disease of,	32	4
Cramps,	2	—	Hemiplegia,	3	—
Cystitis,	3	—	Hernia,	8	1

MEATH HOSPITAL—*continued.*

Diseases.	No. Treated.	No. Died.	Diseases.	No. Treated.	No. Died.
Herpes,	4	—	Poisoning,	4	—
Hydrocele,	2	—	Polypus Nasi,	1	—
Hydrocephalus,	1	1	Prolapsus Ani,	2	—
Hypochondriasis,	2	—	,, Uteri,	4	—
Hysteria,	3	—	Prostate, Enlarged,	3	—
			Prostatitis,	2	—
			Purpura,	3	—
			Pyrosis,	2	—
Influenza,	22	—	Pyræmia,	4	3
			Rectum, Cancer,	2	—
Laryngitis,	4	—	Rheumatism, Acute,	36	—
Lumbago,	3	—	,, Chronic,	24	—
Lupus,	3	—	Rupia,	3	—
Luxation of Humerus,	2	—			
,, Hip,	2	—			
,, Clavicle,	2	—			
			Narcocele,	2	—
			Sciatica,	8	—
Mania,	1	—	Sarcoma,	3	—
Morbus Coxæ,	4	—	Scrofula and Strumæ,	10	1
Marasmus,	4	—	Splenitis,	2	—
Meningitis, Tubercular,	5	6	Sprain,	13	—
			Spine, Curvature of,	2	—
			Stricture of the Œsophagus,	2	—
			,, Urethra,	23	—
Narcosis,	5	—	Synovitis,	2	—
Nephritis,	18	4	Syphilis, Secondary,	2	—
Neuralgia,	3	—	,, Tertiary,	2	—
Neuroma,	1	—			
			Talipes,	3	—
			Tetanus,	2	1
			Tonsillitis,	19	—
Obstruction, Internal,	1	1	Tuberculosis, General,	14	1
Onychia,	2	—	Tumour, Ovarian Cysts,	2	—
Orchitis,	4	—	,, Fatty,	4	—
Osteo-Sarcoma,	2	—	,, Leg,	3	—
Otitis,	3	—			
			Ulcer,	47	—
			Urine, Retention of,	6	—
Paralysis,	3	1	,, Incontinence of,	3	—
Paraplegia,	3	—	,, Infiltration of,	3	—
Paronychia,	3	—	,, Fever,	1	1
Pericarditis,	2	—			
Pericystis,	4	—			
Peritonitis,	3	3			
Pulmonia,	3	—	Varicella,	3	—
Phthisis,	2	—	Variæ,	13	—
Phthisis Pulmonalis,	45	5	Varicocele,	2	—
,, Laryngea,	4	1	Vertigo,	1	—
Pleuritis,	7	1			
Pleuro-pneumonia,	3	1			
Pneumonia,	17	2			
,, Typhoid,	3	—	Wound,	73	—

STEEVENS'S HOSPITAL, Year ended 31st March, 1899.

Disease.	No. Treated.	No. Died.	Disease.	No. Treated.	No. Died.
Abortion,			Fever, Enteric,		2
Abscess,			„ Rheumatic,		
Alcoholism,			Fistula in Ano,		
Amputation,			„ Urethra,		
Asthenia,			Fracture of Leg,		
Acne,			„ Skull,		
Adenitis,			„ Fibula,		
Albuminuria,			„ Tibia,		
Amenorrhœa,			„ Clavicle,		
Anæmia,			„ Patella,		
Aneurism of Aorta,			„ Arm,		
Atrophy of Muscle,			„ Rib,		
Asthma,			„ Toe,		
Ankylosis of Elbow,			„ Femur,		
„ Knee,			„ Humerus,		
„ Hip,			„ Fingers,		
Arthritis,			„ Facial Bones,		
Ascites,			„ Nasal,		
Bronchitis, Acute,			„ Foot,		
„ Chronic,		2	Furuncle,		
Bubo,					
Burns and Scalds,			Genu Valgum,		
Hernia,			Goitre,		
Cancer of Stomach,			Gastritis,		
„ Breast,			Glaucoma,		
„ Parotid Region,			Gonorrhœa,		
„ Lip,					
„ Uterus,			Hæmoptysis,		
„ Liver,			Hæmorrhage,		
„ Jaw,			„ Cerebral,		
Caries of Spine,			Hernia,		
„ Dental,			Hæmorrhoids,		
Catarrh,			Hare Lip,		
Catarrh,			Heart, Disease of,		
Cephalalgia,			Hemiplegia,		
Chancre,			Herpes,		
Chlorosis,			Hydrocele,		
Chorea,			Hyperæmia,		
Catarrh, Internal,			Hysteria,		
Colic,					
Concussion of Brain,			Icterus,		
Conjunctivitis,			Impetigo,		
Constipation,			Inflammation of Jaw,		
Convulsions,			„ Uterus,		
Cramps,			„ Right Foot and Leg,		
Cystitis,			„ Eye,		
Delirium Tremens,					
Disease of Ear,			Influenza,		
Diarrhœa,			Intussusception,		
Diphtheria,			Iritis,		
Dysmenorrhœa,					
Dyspepsia,			Keratitis,		
Dysuria,			Laryngitis,		
Entropion,			Leucorrhœa,		
Eczema,			Lichen,		
Emphysema,			Lithiasis,		
Enteritis,			Lumbago,		
Rheumatism,			Lupus,		
Epilepsy,			Luxation of Hip,		
Epistaxis,			„ Knee,		
Ptosis,			„ Shoulder,		
Erysipelas,			„ Elbow,		
Erythema,			„ Foot,		
Endo-metritis,					

STEEVENS'S HOSPITAL—*continued.*

Disease	No. Treated	No. Died	Disease	No. Treated	No. Died
Malingering,	2	–	Psoriasis,	5	–
Mania,	5	–	Purpura,	1	–
Morbus Coxæ,	5	–	Pharyngitis,	9	–
Mitral Valve, Disease of,	1	1	Pleurisy,	2	–
Myelitis,	1	–	Rachies,	1	–
Meningitis,	4	1	Rheumatism, Acute,	45	–
Myoma Uterus,	1	–	,, Chronic,	4	–
Myopia,	1	–	Sciatica,	3	–
			Scarlatina,	10	–
Necrosis,	2	–	Sarcoma of Eye,	1	–
Nephritis,	9	1	,, Arm,	1	–
Neuralgia,	9	–	Sprains,	28	–
Neurosis,	1	–	Strabismus,	2	–
			Stricture of Urethra,	7	–
Onychia,	2	–	Synovitis,	5	–
Ophthalmia,	3	–	Syphilis, Primary,	28	–
Orchitis,	3	–	,, Secondary,	15	–
Ostitis,	1	–	,, Tertiary,	2	1
Otitis,	3	–	Talipes,	1	–
Ovaritis,	1	–	Tonsillitis,	96	–
			Trachoma,	8	–
Paralysis,	1	–	Tumour,	9	–
Paronychia,	1	–	Tuberculosis of Eye,	1	–
Pernio,	2	–	,, Larynx,	1	–
Periostitis,	3	–	,, Nose,	2	–
Peritonitis,	1	1	,, Hip,	2	–
Phimosis,	5	–	,, Elbow,	1	–
Phthisis Pulmonalis,	43	2	,, Ankle,	2	–
Pleuritis,	2	–	,, Gland,	7	–
Pleurodynia,	1	–	Uterus, Retroflexion of,	5	–
Pneumonia,	11	1	,, Prolapse,	2	–
Polypus Nasi,	5	–	Varix,	33	–
Prolapsus Ani,	2	–	Varicocele,	5	–
Prostate, Enlarged,	1	–	Wounds,	168	–

THE LYING-IN (ROTUNDA) HOSPITAL.

RETURN of DISEASES treated in GYNÆCOLOGICAL (AUXILIARY) WARDS
during Year ended 31st March, 1898.

Disease	No.	Died	Disease	No.	Died
Vulva—			**Vagina—**		
Bartholin Cyst,	4	–	Cystocele only,	2	–
Laceration of Labium			Rectocele only,	6	–
Minus,	1	–	Cystocele and Rectocele,	9	–
Hæmatoma,	1	–	Vaginitis,	11	–
Epithelioma of Clitoris,	1	–	,, Senile,	5	–
			Cyst of Vaginal Wall,	2	–
Perinæum—					
Simple Lacerations,	45	–	**Cervix—**		
Complete Lacerations,	4	–	Lacerations,	52	–
			Hypertrophy,	7	–
Rectum—			Erosions,	4	–
Carcinoma,	3	–	Carcinoma,	11	1
Hæmorrhoids,	4	–	Nabothian Cyst,	1	–
Recto-vaginal Fistula,	1	–	Polypus,	6	–
Prolapse,	1	–			
Ischio-rectal Abscess,	1	–	**Corpus Uteri—**		
			Endometritis & Metritis,	96	1
Urethra and Bladder—			Sub-Involution,	14	–
Caruncle,	6	–	Pathological Ante-		
Vesico-vaginal Fistula,	1	–	flexion,	39	–
Cystitis,	4	–	Threatened Abortion,	8	–

ROTUNDA LYING-IN HOSPITAL.—*continued.*

Disease.	No. Treated.	No. Died.	Disease.	No. Treated.	No. Died.
CORPUS UTERI—con.			**OVARIES—con.**		
Incomplete Abortion,	35	—	Parovarian Cyst,	1	—
Prolapse,	7	—	Prolapse,	7	—
Procidentia,	2	—	**PELVIC PERITONEUM AND**		
Retroversion and Retro-			**CELLULAR TISSUE—**		
flexion,	60	—	Cellulitis and Parame-		
Carcinoma,	1	—	tritis,	3	—
Fibro-Myomata,	23	4	Hæmatocele,	2	—
Hyper-involution,	1	—	Peritonitis,	2	1
Pregnancy,	15	—	Abscess,	1	—
Bicornuate Uterus,	1	—			
			ABDOMEN—		
FALLOPIAN TUBES—			Carcinoma,	8	—
Sacto-salpinx,	2	—	Ventral Hernia,	4	—
Salpingitis,	5	—	Umbilical Epiplocele,	1	—
Tubal Pregnancy,	4	—	Abscess,	3	2
Pyosalpinx,	6	—	Splenic Incency hernia,	1	—
Hæmatosalpinx,	6	—			
Adenoma,	8	—	**MISCELLANEOUS—**		
Tubercular,	8	—	Coccygodynia,	1	—
Hydrosalpinx,	1	1	Calculus in Ureter (?),	1	—
			Mammary Scirrhus,	1	—
OVARIES—			Incontinence of Urine,	6	—
Cyst,	23	1	Bubo,	1	—
Dermoid,	2	—	Mammary Abscess,	1	—
Cirrhosis,	1	—	Phlebitis,	1	—

Board of Dublin Hospitals. 25

Appendix.
No. 1.

Coombe
Lying-in
Hospital

COOMBE LYING-IN HOSPITAL.

RETURN of DISEASES treated in the GYNÆCOLOGICAL WARDS during the Year ended 31st March, 1899.

Abscess of Groin,	1
„ Perinæum,	1
Abortions, Incomplete,	5
Anæmia,	6
Carcinoma of Uterus,	7
„ Cervix,	5
Caruncle,	1
Coccyx, Dislocation of,	1
Constipation,	2
Cystitis,	5
Dysmenorrhœa,	6
Endometritis,	16
Epilepsy,	4
Fibroma of Uterus,	6
Fistula, Recto-vaginal,	1
„ Vesico-vaginal,	1
Gastric Ulcer,	1
Hæmatoma of Vulva,	3
Hæmorrhage, Uterine,	1
Hæmorrhoids,	3
Hernia, Ventral,	1
Hyper-involution,	1
Laceration of Cervix,	8
„ Perinæum,	3
„ Vagina,	2

Mania,	1
Menorrhagia,	5
Metrorrhagia,	6
Nephritis,	1
Neurasthenia,	6
Ovarian Cyst,	5
Ovaritis,	2
Parametritis,	2
Pregnancy,	21
„ Tubal,	3
„ and Varicose Veins,	1
Polypus Uteri,	1
Prolapse of Uterus and Vagina,	6
„ Urethra,	1
Retroflexion and Retroversion,	10
Sapræmia,	1
Stenosis of Cervix,	17
Subinvolution,	7
Vaginitis,	3
Vaginal Cyst,	1
Vulvitis,	7
Varices,	6

RETURN showing the NUMBER of DEATHS in LABOUR WARDS during the Year ended the 31st March, 1899.

No.	Labour Register No.	Age, Years.	Date of Admission.	Date of Delivery.	Date of Death.	Cause of Death.
1	360	44	1898. 7 October,	1898. 2 October,	1898. 3 October,	Accidental Hæmorrhage.
2	245	36	7 October,	7 October,	7 October,	do. do.

Appendix No. 1.
Female Lying-in Hospital.

Return showing Number of **Deaths** in **Gynæcological Wards** during the Year ended 31st March, 1899.

No.	Chronic Regist. No.	Age, Years.	Date of Admission.	Date of Death.	Cause of Death.
1	27	45	14th May, 1898.	29th July, 1898.	Heart Failure after Hysterectomy for Fibro-Myoma.
2	92	31	7th Sept., 1894.	13th Sept., 1898.	Chronic Nephritis.
3	108	41	27th Feb., 1899.	9th March, 1899.	Peritonitis after Hysterectomy.

Royal Hospital for Incurables.

Royal Hospital for Incurables, Year ended 31st March, 1899.

Disease.	No. Treated.	No. Died.	Disease.	No. Treated.	No. Died.
Aneurism of Aorta,	1	–	Hemiplegia,	29	1
Ankylosis of Hip and Knee,	1	–	Hydrocephalus,	1	–
Wrists,	1	–	Hernia,	1	–
Aortic Patency,	2	1			
Arthritis,	29	2			
Asthma,	5	–	Lupus of Face,	8	1
Bronchitis, Chronic,	6	1	Morbus Coxæ,	3	–
			Myelitis,	1	–
			Mitral Valve, Disease of,	8	2
Cancer of Stomach,	1	1			
„ Breast,	8	5	Nephritis,	4	1
„ Uterus,	4	4			
„ Neck or Tongue,	5	3			
„ Face,	4	3	Paralysis (see also Hemiplegia and Paraplegia),	18	8
„ Leg or Arm,	3	1	Paralysis Agitans,	5	–
„ Rectum,	1	–	Paraplegia,	7	–
Caries of Vertebræ,	4	2	Phthisis Pulmonalis,	47	17
„ Bones of Leg,	1	–	Poisoning by Lead,	1	–
„ Pelvis,	1	–			
„ Thigh,	1	–			
Chorea,	1	–	Rachitis,	2	–
Cystitis,	1	–	Rheumatism, Chronic,	18	–
Dropsy,	1	–	Scrofula,	7	–
			Splenitis,	1	–
Eczema,	1	–			
			Tabes,	4	–
Gout,	1	–	Tumour, Ovarian,	1	–
Gastritis,	2	–	„ Uterine,	1	–
			„ Abdominal,	1	–
Hæmorrhoids,	2	–	Uterus, Hypertrophy of,	1	–
Heart, Disease of (see Aortic and Mitral Disease also),	17	3	Ulcer, Rodent,	1	–
			„ Chronic,	1	–

CORK-STREET FEVER HOSPITAL, Year ended 31st March, 1899.

Disease.	No. Treated.	No. Died.	Disease.	No. Treated.	No. Died.
Abscess,	7	—	Laryngitis,	3	1
„ Brain,	1	1	Laryngismus,	3	—
Adenitis,	4	—			
Anæmia,	1	—			
Ague,	1	—	Marasmus,	1	1
Anthrax,	1	1	Meningitis,	16	14
Apoplexy,	1	1			
			Nephritis,	14	4
Bronchitis, Acute,	34	1	Neuralgia,	1	—
Cancer,	2	—	Orchitis,	1	—
Carditis,	1	2	Otitis,	2	—
Cellulitis,	20	—	Observation Cases,	13	—
Cerebral Congestion,	1	—	Ovaritis,	1	—
Catarrh and Pneumonia,	5	1			
Cholera Nostras,	21	4			
Cirrhosis of Liver,	1	—			
Colic,	2	—	Parotitis,	3	—
Congestion of Brain,	1	—	Peritonitis,	1	1
Constipation,	1	—	Pertussis,	22	4
Convulsions,	2	1	Phimosis,	1	—
Croup,	6	1	Phlegmasia Dolens,	2	—
			Phthisis Pulmonalis,	2	2
			Pleuritis,	6	—
Delirium Tremens,	7	2	Pneumonia,	122	31
Dermatitis Gastriforma,	2	—	Plumbism,	1	1
„ Simplex,	1	—	Poisoning by Ptomaines,	1	—
Diarrhœa,	3	2	Pyæmia,	6	6
Diphtheria,	30	15			
Enteritis,	4	—	Renal Congestion,	1	—
Erysipelas,	101	—	Rheumatism, Acute,	32	4
Erythema,	5	—	Rheumatic Purpura,	1	—
Fever, Typhus,	19	7			
„ Enteric,	302	85			
„ Simple,	14	—			
„ Measles,	19	—	Scarlatina,	438	31
„ Rötheln,	19	—	Septicæmia,	10	3
„ Puerperal,	3	1	Sudamina,	1	—
			Stomatitis,	6	—
Furuncle,	1	—			
			Tonsillitis,	36	—
Gangrene of Leg,	1	1	Tabes Mesenterica,	4	—
Cachexia,	1	—	Tuberculosis,	4	5
Gastritis,	8	1	Typhlitis,	4	—
Gastro-Enteritis,	1	—			
Hæmoptysis,	2	—	Urticaria,	1	—
Hemiplegia,	1	—	Ulcerated Throat,	5	—
Hypochondriasis,	1	—	„ Leg,	1	—
Hysteria,	1	—			
			Varicella,	9	—
Injury,	2	—			
Insane,	6	—			
Tetanus,	55	—	Minders,	48	—

WESTMORELAND LOCK HOSPITAL, Year ended 31st March, 1898.

Disease.	No. Treated.	No. Died.	Disease.	No. Treated.	No. Died.
Abortion,	2	-	Neuritis,	1	-
Abscess, Ischio-Rectal,	3	-	Nil,	11	-
Labial,	7	-			
Atresiohilum,	2	-			
Adenitis, Cervical,	1	-			
Inguinal,	4	-	Ophthalmia Neonatorum,	2	-
Multiple,	4	-	Ovaritis,	1	-
Arthritis of Knee,	3	-			
			Parotitis,	3	-
			Pediculi Capitis,	2	-
Bronchitis, Acute,	5	-	Periostitis,	1	-
Bubo,	3	-	Pelvoois, Inflammatory,	1	-
			Phthisis pulmonalis,	5	6
			Pirsonitoria,	1	-
Cachexia Syphilitica,	4	-	Pneumonia,	2	-
Cephalalgia,	3	-	Pruritus,	5	-
Chancroid,	44	-	Pregnancy,	17	-
Cirrhosis of Lung,	3	-	Prurigo,	4	-
Condyloma,	35	-			
Cynanche,	2	-			
			Rheumatism, Chronic,	8	-
Dysuria,	2	-			
			Scabies,	22	-
			Scirrhus,	1	-
Eczema,	1	-	Serpiginous,	1	-
Endometritis,	1	-	Syphilis, Congenital,	5	4
Erythema Nodosum,	2	-	Infantile,	2	2
Excoriation,	2	-	Primary,	40	-
			Secondary,	68	-
			Tertiary,	35	1
Fissure,	3	-			
Anal,	7	-	Tonsillitis,	3	-
Gastritis,	3	-			
Glans,	15	-			
Gonorrhœa,	73	-	Ulcer of Foot,	2	-
			Hand,	1	-
Hæmorrhoids,	3	-	Tubercular,	3	-
Rem Iemala,	2	-	Syphilitic,	3	-
Hernia Irida,	1	-	Toe,	2	-
			Tonsil,	1	-
			Vaginal,	1	-
Injury to Elbow,	1	-	Os Uteri,	3	-
Knee,	1	-	Ulcerative Phagedæna,	4	-
Influenza,	3	-	Urethritis,	1	-
			Urethral Caruncle,		
Labial Hypertrophy,	14	-			
Leucorrhœa,	6	-	Vaginitis,	2	-
			Vulvitis,	3	-
			Verruca,	1	-
Menorrhagia,	2	-			
Mitral Valve, Disease of,	1	-			
Molluscum,	3	-	Wound on Arm,	3	-

ROYAL VICTORIA EYE AND EAR HOSPITAL.

(ST. MARK'S BRANCH.)

DISEASES of NEW PATIENTS treated during the Year ending 31st December, 1899.

EYE DISEASES,—

Diseases of the Eyelids,		517
Do.	Conjunctiva,	1,508
Do.	Cornea,	1,028
Do.	Sclerotic,	74
Do.	Uveal Tract,	250
Do.	Vitreous,	19
Do.	Retina and Optic Nerve,	113
Do.	Globe,	52
Do.	Lens,	508
Do	Muscles and Nerves,	145
Do.	Orbit,	14
Do.	Lacrimal Apparatus,	66
Glaucoma,		25
Errors of Refraction and Accommodation,		550
		4,800
Ear Diseases,		1,504
Nose and Throat Diseases,		53
Unclassified,		43
		5,900

TABLE No. 2, showing the AVERAGE COST per BED occupied throughout the Year ended 31st MARCH, 1899, for MAINTENANCE, and for ESTABLISHMENT, and for both, exclusive of Buildings and furnishing such Buildings.

NAME OF HOSPITAL.	Average daily number of Beds occupied throughout the year.	Average annual cost per bed for Maintenance.	Average annual cost per bed for Establishment, exclusive of buildings and furnishing such buildings, and Incidentals.	Average annual cost per bed for Maintenance and for Establishment, exclusive of buildings and furnishing such buildings, and Incidentals.
		£ s. d.	£ s. d.	£ s. d.
Westmoreland Lock,	60·67	29 12 11	30 5 1½	39 4 8½
Steevens's,	105·72	25 0 5	33 18 4½	58 19 9½
Meath,	93·12	22 13 8½	34 9 10½	54 3 7½
Cork-street Fever,	165·31	34 9 6½	30 8 6½	44 2 1½
House of Industry,	144·15	24 13 0	34 5 9½	49 18 9½
Rotunda Lying-in,	70·82	19 18 3	54 2 2½	73 1 5½
Coombe do.,	27·87	21 5 9½	62 14 0½	84 1 9½
Incurables,	210·1	19 19 8½	17 5 1½	36 4 9½
Royal Victoria Eye and Ear,	99·	15 10 9½	22 7 2	38 3 11½

* Maintenance comprises provisions, groceries, alcoholic stimulants, drugs, leeches, surgical instruments, medical appliances, and clothing of patients.

† Establishment charges include salaries of officers, wages of servants, rations of officers and servants, clothing of servants, rent, taxes, insurance, soap, candles, fuel, gas-light, furniture, repairs, stores, buildings, utensils, buildings, and furnishing such buildings, stationery, printing, advertising, burials, coffins, pensions, incidentals, and laundry expenses.

Appendix.
No. 1.
Royal Victoria Eye and Ear Hospital.

Appendix.
No. 2.
Average cost per Bed, 1899.

Appendix.
No. 3.
Expenses of Hospitals.

TABLE No. 3, showing in detail the several Chief Heads of Expenditure of
and to Establishment, and the

EXPENDITURE FOR MAINTENANCE FOR

Name of Hospital.	Provisions.	Groceries.	Establishment.			Drugs and Leeches.	Surgical Instruments and other Medicines and Surgical Appliances.
			Wine.	Whiskey, Brandy, &c., and Porter.	Ale and Porter.		
	£ s. d.	£ s. d.	£ s. d.	£ s. d.	£ s. d.	£ s. d.	£ s. d.
Westmoreland Lock,							
Steevens's,							
Meath,							
Cork-street,							
House of Industry,							
Kssmds Lying-in,							
Coombe do.							
Incurables,							
Royal Victoria Eye and Ear,							
Totals,							

EXPENDITURE FOR ESTABLISHMENT FOR

Name of Hospital.	Rent, Taxes, and Insurance.	Soap and Candles.	Coals and other Fuel, and Gas Light.	Furniture and Repairs.	Straw, Bedding, and Utensils.	Buildings, and Furnishing and Repairing Buildings.	For Money, Printing and Advertising, &c.
	£ s. d.	£ s. d.	£ s. d.	£ s. d.	£ s. d.	£ s. d.	£ s. d.
Westmoreland Lock,							
Steevens's,							
Meath,							
Cork-street,							
House of Industry,							
Kssmds Lying-in,							
Coombe do.							
Incurables,							
Royal Victoria Eye and Ear,							
Totals,							

* Includes £3,450 for Nurses' home, and £739 114 8½ for new laundry.   † Includes £320

each Hospital, in the Year ended 31st March, 1839, in respect to Maintenance,
Total Expenditure for Maintenance.

Clothing of Patients.	Total Maintenance.	Salaries of Officers.	Wages of Servants.	Rations of Officers and Servants.	Clothing of Servants.	Name of Hospital.
£ s. d.	£ s. d.	£ s. d.	£ s. d.	£ s. d.	£ s. d.	
0 1 5	722 11 1	725 6 6	311 15 1	163 5 10	23 1 4	Westmoreland Lock.
—	2,623 6 10	401 16 2	954 16 11	734 6 11	—	Steevens's.
—	2,113 10 3	431 10 0	501 10 14	983 11 7	74 14 6	Meath.
172 5 0	2,316 3 6	728 10 7	636 3 3	227 13 3	—	Cork-street.
—	2,184 20 11	790 17 0	1,340 2 0	620 17 7	67 5 0	House of Industry.
12 14 10	1,342 10 0	172 3 11	447 18 7	246 16 11	24 10 0	Rotunda Lying-in.
4 17 1	634 16 0	761 4 0	723 5 8	630 6 0	6 10 1	Coombe do.
60 15 0	3,356 17 0	301 11 10	647 16 0	—	—	Incurables.
—	1,701 17 11	640 1 7	263 4 4	179 17 6	17 16 3	Royal Victoria Eye and Ear.
266 3 9	17,723 7 6	4,421 3 11	5,580 2 6	4,664 11 0	196 13 9	Totals.

Portrix and Eating.	Potatoes.	Incidentals.	Laundry Expenses.	Total Establishment.	Total Expenditure.	Name of Hospital.
£ s. d.	£ s. d.	£ s. d.	£ s. d.	£ s. d.	£ s. d.	
13 10 0	40 10 0	90 17 0	—	1,497 13 11	2,783 0 3	Westmoreland Lock.
—	—	147 16 11	—	2,033 0 3	10,56 1 7	Steevens's.
10 1 0	—	340 18 0	—	2,162 10 0	5,770 0 1	Meath.
30 0 1	24 10 0	634 4 8	—	4,301 1 6	7,634 4 4	Cork-street.
3 14 0	763 1 0	170 17 0	—	14,560 10 7	12,157 11 6	House of Industry.
—	10 0 0	427 10 0	301 10 0	4,736 3 7	4,081 7 3	Rotunda Lying-in.
—	—	60 73 1	67 6 1	1,151 3 3	1,721 10 3	Coombe do.
—	—	2,903 0 11	—	2,310 6 0	5,830 7 3	Incurables.
—	—	92 11 4	107 0 3	1,546 0 0	2,511 1 1	Royal Victoria Eye and Ear.
60 11 10	838 14 0	4,391 10 0	651 13 2	40,744 14 7	60,870 1 1	Totals.

Invested in Stock.   ‡ Includes £1,800 on Investments, and £78 6s. 11d. for out-patients, &c.

Table No. 1.

Showing the annual Number of Tons of each Mineral, in the Year ended 31st March, 1877.

Table No. 4, showing the Number of Patients treated in each Institution under the Supervision of the Board of Supervision of the Public Hospitals in the Year ended 31st March, 18__; also Mortality in each; the Average Daily Number in Hospital during the Year; and the present extent of Accommodation for each class of Patients.

Appendix.
No. 8.
Price List.

PRICE LIST of ARTICLES supplied to the HOUSE OF INDUSTRY GOVERNMENT HOSPITALS, per Contract or otherwise, for the Year ending 31st March, 1899.

Articles		Rate.			Remarks.
		£	s.	d.	
1. Beef,	per lb.	0	0	3½	
2. Mutton,	"	0	0	7	
3. Bacon,	"	0	0	4½	
4. Bread,	"	0	0	1½	
5. Potatoes,	per stone,	0	0	8½	
6. Oatmeal,	"	0	1	0	
7. Rice,	"	0	1	7	
8. Tea,	per lb.	0	3	3	
9. Sugar,	"	0	0	1½	
10. Coffee,	"	0	1	7	
11. Cocoa,	"		—		
12. New Milk,	per gal.	0	0	9	
13. Buttermilk,	"	0	0	2	
14. Brandy,	"	1	1	0	
15. Whiskey,	"	1	0	0	
16. Wine, {Port,	"	0	8	0	
{Marsala,	"	0	7	0	
17. Porter,	per ½ brl.	0	6	6	
18. Butter,	per lb.	0	1	0	
19. Eggs,	per doz.	0	1	0	
20. Soap (White),	per cwt.	0	15	6	
21. Coals,	per ton,	0	15	6	

PRICE LIST of ARTICLES supplied to the MEATH HOSPITAL, per Contract or otherwise, for the Year ending 31st March, 1899.

Article.		Rate.			Remarks.
		£	s.	d.	
1. Beef {Soup, &c.,	per lb	0	0	4½	
{Roasting,	"	0	0	7	
2. Mutton,	"	0	0	7	
3. Bacon,	"	0	0	7½	
4. Bread,	"		—		Current shop prices, 10 per cent. discount off.
5. Oatmeal,	per stone,	0	1	7	
6. Potatoes,	"	0	0	8	Average Market prices.
7. Rice,	"	0	2	3	
8. Tea,	per lb.	0	1	8	
9. Sugar,	per cwt.	0	15	0	
10. Coffee,	per lb.	0	1	6	
11. Cocoa (patent),	per tin,	0	0	6	
12. New Milk,	per gal.	0	0	8	
13. Buttermilk,	"	0	0	2	
14. Whiskey,	"	0	18	6	
15. Brandy,	"	0	19	6	
16. Wine (Port),	"				
17. Porter,	per ½ brl.	0	19	0	Guinness's XX.
18. Butter,	per lb.	0	0	11½	Average.
19. Eggs,	per doz.	0	0	11½	Do.
20. Soap {(Brown),	per cwt.	0	11	6	
{(White),	"	0	13	0	
21. Candles,	per lb.	0	0	5½	
22. Coal,	per ton,	0	14	0	

PRICE LIST of ARTICLES supplied to the ROTUNDA LYING-IN HOSPITAL, per Contract or otherwise, for the Year ending 31st March, 1699.

Article.		Rate. £ s. d.	Remarks.
1. Beef,	per lb.	—	
2. Mutton,	„	—	
3. Bacon,	„		
4. Bread,	per 2 lb. loaf,	0 0 5½	
5. Oatmeal,	per cwt	0 0 2½	
6. Potatoes,	per stone,	0 12 0	
7. Rice,	„	5d. to 9d.	
8. Tea,	per lb.	0 1 7	
9. Sugar	{Moist per stone	0 1 4	
	{Lump, „	0 1 7	
10. Coffee	per lb.	0 3 4	
11. Cocoa,	per ½ lb. tin,	0 1 6	
12. New Milk,	per gal.	0 0 10	
13. Buttermilk,		0 0 8	
14. Whiskey,	per quart,	0 5 0	
15. Brandy,		—	
16. Wine,		—	
17. Porter,		—	
18. Butter,	per lb.	{0 0 10	Whiteside.
		{0 1 0	Lipton.
19. Eggs,	per 120	0 10 6	
20. Soap	{Brown, per cwt.	0 16 0	
	{White, „	0 16 0	
	{Carbolic „	1 14 0	
21. Candles,	per packet,	0 2 0	
22. Coals,			

PRICE LIST of ARTICLES supplied to the COOMBE LYING-IN HOSPITAL per Contract or otherwise, for the Year ending 31st March, 1899.

Article.		Rate. £ s. d.	Remarks.
1. Beef,	per lb.	0 0 7	
2. Mutton,	„	0 0 7	
3. Bacon,	„	0 0 7	
4. Bread,	per 2 lb. loaf,	—	One half-penny off current price.
5. Oatmeal,	per stone,	0 2 0	
6. Potatoes,	„	0 0 8	
7. Rice,	„	—	
8. Tea,	per lb.	0 1 4	
9. Sugar,	„	0 0 1½	
10. Coffee,	„	0 1 10	
11. Cocoa,		—	
12. New Milk,	per gal.	0 0 8½	
13. Buttermilk,	„	0 0 3	
14. Whiskey,	„	0 16 8	
15. Brandy,	per flask,	0 5 0	
16. Wine,		—	
17. Porter,		—	
18. Butter,	per lb.	0 1 0	
19. Eggs,	per doz.	0 1 0	
20. Soap,	per stone,	2s. 6d. and 8s.	
21. Candles,		—	
22. Coals,	per ton.	0 15 0	

Appendix.
No. 2.
Price Lists

Price List of Articles supplied to the Royal Hospital for Incurables, per Contract or otherwise, for the Year ending 31st March, 1899.

Article.		Rate.	Remarks.
		£ s. d.	
1. Beef,	per lb.	0 0 7½	Loins of beef, legs of mutton, and steak.
„	„	0 0 7	Tail ends and rounds of beef.
„ Neck,	„	0 0 6	
2. Necks of mutton,	„	0 0 4½	
3. Bacon,	per cwt.	3 0 0	
4. Bread,	per 2 lb. loaf,	0 0 2½	
5. Oatmeal,	per cwt.,	0 14 6	
6. Potatoes,	per ton,	3 5 0	Average.
7. Rice,	per stone,	0 4 0	
8. Tea,	per lb.	0 1 8	
9. Sugar,	per stone,	0 3 0	
10. Coffee,	per lb.	0 1 10	
11. Cocoa (shell),	„	0 0 4½	
12. New Milk,	per gal.	0 0 8	
13. Buttermilk,	„	—	No charge.
14. Whiskey,	„	0 13 4	
15. Brandy,	per bottle,	—	Not used.
16. Wine, "Marsala,"	„	0 1 4	
„ Port, per qr. cask,		9 10 0	
17. Porter,	per ½ bar.	0 13 4	
18. Butter,	per lb.	0 1 1½	Average price.
19. Eggs (new laid),	per doz.	0 1 3	
„ (cooking),	per 120	0 8 6	
20. Soap, X.X.P.C.,	per cwt.	1 0 0	
„ X.X Brown,	„	0 14 0	
21. Candles,	„	—	Not used.
22. Coals, Wigan,	per ton,	0 13 0	
23. Steam Slack,	„	0 9 0	

Price List of Articles supplied to the Cork-street Fever Hospital, per Contract or otherwise, for the Year ending 31st March, 1899.

Article.		Rate.	Remarks.
		£ s. d	
1. Beef,	per lb.	6½d. and 7d.	
2. Mutton,	„	6½d. and 7d.	
3. Bacon,	„	6d. and 6d.	
4. Bread,	per 2 lb. loaf,	3d. and 3½d.	
5. Oatmeal,	„	—	No Contract.
6. Potatoes,	„	—	No Contract.
7. Rice,	„	—	No Contract.
8. Tea,	per lb.	0 1 8	
9. Sugar,	per cwt.	0 17 0	
10. Coffee,	„	—	No Contract.
11. Cocoa,	„	—	
12. New Milk,	per gal.	7½d. and 8d.	
13. Buttermilk,	„	0 0 3	
14. Whiskey,	„	0 11 0	
15. Brandy,	per bot.	0 6 0	
16. Wine,	„	0 3 0	
17. Porter,	per d doz. large	1 1 0	
18. Butter,	„	—	Wholesale Market Price.
19. Eggs,	per doz.	—	Wholesale Market Price.
20. Soap,	„	—	Wholesale Market Price.
21. Candles,	„	—	Wholesale Market Price.
22. Coals,	per ton,	0 15 6	Average.
23. Do., Steam,	„	0 14 9	

PRICE LIST of ARTICLES supplied to the WESTMORLAND LOCK (GOVERN-
MENT) HOSPITAL, per Contract or otherwise, for the Year ending 31st
March, 1899.

Appendix.
No. 4
Price Lists

Article.		Rate.	Remarks.
		£ s. d.	
1. Beef,	per lb.	0 0 5½	
2. Mutton,	„	0 0 6|	
3. Bacon	„	0 0 6½	
4. Bread,	„	0 0 1½	Equal to 5d. per 4 lb. loaf.
5. Oatmeal,	per cwt.	0 14 0	
6. Potatoes,	per stone,	0 0 7	
7. Rice,	per lb.	0 0 1½	
8. Tea,	„	0 1 8	
9. Sugar,	„	0 0 1½	
10. Coffee,		—	Not in dietary.
11. Cocoa,		—	
12. New Milk,	per gal.	0 0 7½	
13. Buttermilk,	„	0 0 2½	
14. Whiskey,	„	0 18 6	
15. Brandy,	per flask,	0 5 7	
16. Porter,	{in wood, per ½ brl.	0 13 4	
	in bottle, „ doz.	0 1 4	
17. Wine,	{Marsala, per gal.	0 7 0	
	Port, per bot.	0 3 0	
18. Butter,	per lb.	0 0 10	
19. Eggs,	per doz.	0 0 10	
20. Soap,	{Crown, per cwt.	0 18 0	
	Brown „	0 14 6	
21. Candles,	{Paraffin, per lb.	0 0 8	
	Wax, „	0 2 0	
21. Coal,	per ton,	0 13 6	
22. Coke,	„	0 16 0	

PRICE LIST of ARTICLES supplied to the ROYAL VICTORIA EYE AND
EAR HOSPITAL, per Contract or otherwise, for the year ending
31st March, 1899.

Article.		Rate.	Remarks.
		£ s. d.	
1. Beef,	per lb.	0 0 7	
2. Mutton,	„	0 0 7	
3. Bacon (Limerick),	„	0 0 8	Current price, less 17½ p. cent. disct.
4. Bread,		—	Little used.
5. Oatmeal,	per stone,	0 2 4	Current Market Price.
6. Potatoes,		—	
7. Rice,	per lb.	0 0 2½	
8. Tea,	„	0 1 3	
9. Sugar,	per stone,	0 1 6	
10. Coffee,		—	Seldom used.
11. Cocoa,		—	
12. New Milk,	per gal.	0 0 8½	
13. Buttermilk,	„	—	None.
14. Whiskey,		—	
15. Brandy,		—	Very seldom used—no Contract.
17. Wine,		—	
18. Porter,		—	
18. Butter (Fresh),	per lb	0 1 0	All the year.
19. Eggs,	per doz.	0 1 0	„ „
20. Soap,	per stone,	0 2 0	
21. Candles,		—	Little used.
22. Coals,	per ton,	—	About 10s. per cent. under current cash price.

PRICE LIST of ARTICLES supplied to STEEVENS'S HOSPITAL, per Contract or otherwise, for the Year ending 31st March, 1899.

Article.		Rate.	Remarks.
		£. s. d.	
1. Beef,	per lb.	2½, 4d., 6d.	For legs, necks, and rounds.
2. Mutton,	,,	0 0 6½	
3. Bacon,	,,	0 0 7½	
4. Bread,	per 2 lb. loaf,	0 0 3½	
5. Oatmeal,	per cwt.	0 15 0	
6. Potatoes,	,,	0 4 5	
7. Rice,	per stone,	0 2 0½	
8. Tea,	per lb.	0 1 4	
9. Sugar,	,,	0 0 1½	
10. Coffee,	,,	0 1 6	
11. Cocoa,			
12. New Milk,	per gal.	0 0 7½	
13. Buttermilk,	,,	0 0 2	
14. Whiskey,	,,	0 16 0	
15. Brandy,	,,	1 5 0	
16. Wine, Port,	per doz.	1 0 0	
17. Porter,	per ½ cask,	0 18 6	
18. Butter,	per lb.	0 0 10½	
19. Eggs,	per 120	0 9 0	
20. Soap, Brown,	per cwt.	0 19 6	
21. Candles, Wax,	per doz.	0 3 0	
22. Coals,	per ton,	0 15 3	Best screened 6 foot Wigan.

TABLE No. 7.—DIETARIES.

WESTMORLAND LOCK HOSPITAL.

Diets.	Breakfast.	Dinner.	Supper.
Low Diet.	Bread, 4 oz. Tea, ½ pint.	Bread, 4 oz. New Milk, ½ pint. On Friday—Bread, 4 oz.; New Milk, ½ pint; Gruel, ½ pint.	Bread, 4 oz. Tea, ½ pint. Whey, ½ pint.
Middle Diet.	Bread, 4 oz. Tea, ½ pint.	Bread, 4 oz. or Potatoes, 1 lb. Mutton (leg), roast or boiled, 4 oz. On Friday—Bread, 4 oz.; Gruel, ½ pint, instead of Mutton.	Bread, 4 oz. Tea, ½ pint.
Full Diet.	Bread, 8 oz. Tea, ½ pint.	Bread, 4 oz. or Potatoes, 1 lb. Beef, boiled or stewed, 8 oz., and broth, ½ pint. On Friday—Bread, 4 oz.; Gruel, ½ pint, instead of Potatoes, Beef, &c.	Bread, 4 oz. Tea, ½ pint.
Children's Diet.	N. Milk, 1 pt. Bread, 8 oz. (daily.)	Extras, if prescribed.	
Admission Diet.	Each Adult Patient to get on day of Admission, Dinner, Bread, 8 oz.; Supper, Bread, 4 oz.		

EXTRAS ALLOWED if specially prescribed WITH THE UNDERMENTIONED DIETS.
Low Diet.—One Egg; Beef Tea, ½ pint, or New Milk, ½ pint, or Arrowroot, ½ pint, or Rice Milk, ½ pint. Wine, or Whiskey, or Gin, as specially prescribed.
Middle Diet.—Bread, 4 oz.; 1 Egg; New Milk, ½ pint, or Porter, ½ pint, or Gin or Wine, Whiskey or Brandy, as prescribed.
Full Diet.—Bread 4 oz.; 1 Egg; New Milk, ½ pint, or Porter, ½ pint, or Wine, Whiskey, or Brandy, as prescribed.
Children's Diet.—Bread, 4 oz.; New Milk, ½ pint; Arrowroot or Sago, 1 oz. Sugar with A or N, 4 oz.; or Beef Tea, ½ pint.

Appendix No. I. Dietaries.

FORMULARIES.

Tea (6½ pints).	Beef, with Broth (6½ pints).	Beef Tea (12 pints).
Tea, . . . 1½ oz. Sugar, . . . 4 oz. New Milk, . . [illegible] pt. Allowance for each Patient per diem— Tea for Bkt., [illegible] oz. } [illegible] oz. „ Supr. [illegible] oz. } Sugar Bkt., [illegible] oz. } 1 oz. „ Supr. [illegible] oz. } New Milk, . . [illegible] pt.	Beef, exclusive of bone, 4 lbs. Barley, . . . [illegible] lb. Oatmeal, . . . 1 oz. Parsley, . . . 1 oz. Thyme, . . . [illegible] oz. Onions or Leeks, . . [illegible] lb. Pepper and Salt to taste.	Beef (lean without bone), 8 lbs. Pepper and Salt to taste. Allowance for each Patient— Beef to make [illegible] pt. B. T., 12 oz.
Whey (8¾ pints).	**Gruel (6¾ pints).**	**Arrowroot or Rice Milk (1 pint).**
New Milk, 2 quarts. Butter Milk, 1 quart. Allowance for Whey each Patient— New Milk, . . [illegible] pt. Buttermilk, . . [illegible] pt.	Oatmeal . . . 12 oz. Sugar . . . . 4 oz. Ginger to flavour. Steep the meal from night before. Boil for two hours. Allowance for each Patient for Gruel— Oatmeal . . . 1½ oz. Sugar . . . . [illegible] oz.	Arrowroot or Rice, . . 2 oz. Sugar, ... [illegible] oz. New Milk, . . . [illegible] pt.

Breakfast at Nine o'clock, A.M., Dinner at Two o'clock, P.M., Supper at Seven o'clock, P.M.

RICHMOND, WHITWORTH, and HARDWICKE HOSPITALS.

Diets.	Breakfast.	Luncheon.	Dinner.	Tea.	Supper.
Low,	Tea, 1 pint; bread and butter, 6 oz. and egg.	Milk, 1 pint; bread, 2 oz.	Milk pudding or beef-tea.	Bread and butter 8 oz.; tea, with milk and sugar, 1 pint.	Bread and milk or gruel.
MIDDLE: Sun., .	Bread and butter, 8 oz.; tea, with milk and sugar, 1 pint.	Bread, 6 oz.; milk, 1 pint.	Roast mutton, [illegible] lb.; potatoes, 1 lb.; and vegetables.	Tea, 1 pint, with milk and sugar; bread, 6 oz.	Bread and milk or porridge.
Mon., .	do.	do.	Stewed beef, [illegible] lb.; potatoes, 1 lb.; soup, 1 pint; and cabbage.	do.	do.
Tues., .	do.	do.	Boiled mutton, [illegible] lb.; potatoes, 1 lb., and turnips.	do.	do.
Wed., .	do.	do.	Roast beef, [illegible] lb.; potatoes, 1 lb.	do.	do.
Thurs., .	do.	do.	Irish stew, . .	do.	do.
Frid., .	do.	do.	Beef or mutton, [illegible] lb. each; potatoes, 1 lb.	do.	do.
Sat., .	do.	do.	Roast mutton, [illegible] lb.; potatoes, 1 lb.; and vegetables.	do.	do.

Appendix.
No. 2.
Dietaries.

COKE-STREET FEVER HOSPITAL.

Table of Diets.

Diets	Break'fast.	Lunch.	Dinner.	Tea.
Adults—				
1. Full,	Bread, 4 oz.; tea, 1 pint; milk, ½ pint; egg, 1.	Broth, ½ pint; bread, 4 oz.	Meat, 8 oz.; potatoes, 1 lb.	Bread, 4 oz.; butter, ½ oz.; tea, 1 pint; milk, ½ pint.
2. Middle,	Bread, 4 oz.; tea, 1 pint; milk, ½ pint; egg, 1.	Broth, 1 pint; bread, 3 oz.	Bread, 8 oz.; beef tea, ½ pint.	Bread, 4 oz.; butter, ½ oz.; tea, 1 pint; milk, ½ pint.
3. Low,	Tea, ½ pint; milk, 1½ pints.	—	Beef tea, 1 pint.	Milk, 1½ pints.
Children—				
1. Full,	Bread, 4 oz.; tea, 1 pint; milk, ½ pint; egg, 1.	Broth, ½ pint; bread, 2 oz.	Meat, 4 oz.; potatoes, ½ lb.	Bread, 4 oz.; butter, ½ oz.; tea, ½ pint; milk, ½ pint.
2. Middle,	Bread, 3 oz.; tea, 1 pint; milk, ½ pint; egg, 1.	do.	Bread, ½ lb.; beef tea, ½ pint.	Bread, 3 oz.; butter, ½ oz.; tea, ½ pint; milk, ½ pint.
3. Low,	Milk, 1 pint.	—	Beef tea, ½ pint.	Milk, 1 pint.

Extras as ordered by the Medical Officers.

Quantities per diem allowed to each Patient according to above Table.

Articles	Full Diet.	Middle.	Low.	Articles	Full Diet.	Middle.	Low.
Adults—				**Children—**			
Bread oz.	16	12	—	Bread oz.	10	8	—
Butter "	½	½	½	Butter "	½	½	—
Tea "	⅛	⅛	⅛	Tea "	⅛	⅛	⅛
Milk pt.	1	1½	2	Milk pt.	1½	1½	1
Sugar oz.	2	2	2	Sugar oz.	1½	1½	1
Meat or Fish, "	8	—	—	Meat and Fish, "	4	—	—
Potatoes lb.	1	—	—	Potatoes lb.	½	—	—
Beef Tea pts.	—	½	1	Beef Tea pts.	—	½	½
Eggs "	1	1	1	Eggs "	1	1	1

DOCTOR STEEVENS'S HOSPITAL.

DIETARY LIST.

FULL DIETS—BREAKFAST.

1 pint Tea, 8 oz. Bread, ½ oz. Butter.

DINNER.

Sunday, Tuesday, Thursday,	Roast or Boiled Mutton, 6 oz.; Vegetables, 1 lb. Potatoes.
Monday, Wednesday, Saturday,	1 pint Soup, 6 oz. Stewed Beef, and 1 lb. Potatoes.
Friday,	16 oz. Fish, and 1 lb. Potatoes.
Lunch,	1 pint broth, and 2 oz. Bread.
Tea,	1 pint Tea, ½ oz. Butter, and 4 oz. Bread.
Supper,	1 pint Milk.

EXTRA DIETS.

Pea' Tea, Chops, Chickens, Milk, Eggs, Fish, Jellies, Puddings, Cocoa, Coffee, Porridge, and Stimulants, as ordered by Physicians and Surgeons.

COOMBE LYING-IN HOSPITAL.

No Extras allowed unless ordered each day and initialled by one of the Medical Officers.

Diets.	Breakfast.	Dinner and Luncheon.	Supper.
No. 1,	Tea, 1 pint. Bread, 4 oz.	Luncheon—Milk, ½ pint. Mutton, ½ lb.; bread, 4 oz.; or head soup, 1 pint.	Tea, 1 pint; bread, 4 oz. Supper—Milk, 1 pint, or gruel, 1 pint.
No. 2,	Tea, 1 pint. Bread, 4 oz.	Luncheon—Milk, ½ pint. Ox-head soup, 1 pint; bread, 4 oz.; whey, 1 pint, 4 o'clock.	Tea, 1 pint; bread, 4 oz. Supper—Gruel, 1 pint, containing ½ pint milk.
No. 3,	Tea, 1 pint. Bread, 4 oz.	Luncheon—Milk, 1 pint. Special beef tea, 1 pint; whey or milk, 1 pint, 4 o'clock.	Tea, 1 pint; bread, 4 oz. Supper—Milk, 1 pint.
No. 4,		SLOP DIET IN 24 HOURS:— Special beef tea, ... 2 pints. Milk, ... 4 pints.	

Breakfast, 7.30 A.M.; Luncheon, 11 A.M.; Dinner, 1 P.M.; Tea, 5 and 6 P.M.; Supper, 8.30 P.M.

EXTRAS AND STIMULANTS AS ORDERED IN ALL DIETS.

Tea, ½ lb.; sugar, 1 lb.; milk, 2 pints—supplies 10 patients for 24 hours.
Bread, 2 lbs. loaf—6 lbs. supplies 6 patients for 24 hours.
Ox-head broth—½ ox-head for broth, thickened with barley and dried vegetables, for 10 patients.
Special beef tea—gravy beef, ½ lb. to 1 pint.
Whey—milk, ½ pint, and buttermilk, ½ pint, to make 1 pint.
Gruel—oatmeal, 1 oz., to milk, ½ pint, for 1 pint.

MEATH HOSPITAL.

PATIENTS' DIETARY.

The Patients' Dietary has been revised, and the following recommended on the 11th February, 1863, to be tried for three months, and if approved then to be permanently adopted:—

FULL DIET—BREAKFAST.
Tea, with Milk and Sugar, 1 pint, Bread, with Butter, 4 oz.

DINNER.

Sunday, . . .	Roast Legs of Mutton, 8 oz., with Vegetables and Potatoes.
Monday, . .	Stewed Beef, 8 oz., Soup, 1 pint, and Potatoes.
Tuesday, . .	Boiled Legs of Mutton, 8 oz., and Potatoes.
Wednesday, .	Stewed Beef, 8 oz., Soup, 1 pint, and Potatoes.
Thursday, . .	Roast Legs of Mutton, 8 oz., with Vegetables and Potatoes.
Friday, . .	White Fish, 16 oz., and Potatoes.
Saturday, . .	Stewed Beef, 8 oz., Soup, 1 pint, and Potatoes.
Tea, . . .	Tea, with Sugar and Milk, 1 pint, Bread, with Butter, 4 oz., or Oatmeal Porridge, 16 oz., and New Milk, 1 pint.
Supper, . .	Milk or Whey, 1 pint.

FEVER DIET.

Per Diem, . . . Milk, Barley-Water, Beef Tea, &c., as ordered by Physician.

SPECIAL DIET.

Breakfast, . .	Same as Full Diet.
Dinner, . .	As ordered by Physician or Surgeon.
Tea, . .	Same as Full Diet.
Supper, . .	Ditto.

The Medical Attendant can order, when necessary, Beef Tea, Milk, Eggs, Chop, Fowl, Fish, Rice, Puddings, Fruit, Cocoa, Ice, Mineral Waters, Stimulants, &c.; but they will be given only when signed for by him.

FORMULARIES.

Tea (1½ pints).	Boiled Beef with Broth (1¼ pints).	Beef Tea (¼ pints).
Tea, . . 2 oz. Sugar, . . 4 oz. New Milk, ½ pint.	Beef (exclusive of bone), 6 lb. Onions or Leeks, . ½ lb. Pepper and Salt to taste.	Beef (lean, without bone), 4 lb. Pepper and Salt to taste. **Whey.** New Milk, . . . 1 quart. Buttermilk, . . . 1 pint.

Gruel (½ pints).	Arrowroot (1 pint).	Warm Milk.	Rice Milk (½ pints).
Oatmeal, . 3 oz. Salt, . . 2 oz. Steep the meal from night before, boil for two hours.	New Milk, . 1 pint. Arrowroot, . . ½ oz. Sugar, . . ½ oz.	New Milk, . 3 pints. Boiling Water, 1 pint.	Rice, . . 6 oz. Sugar, . . 2 oz. New Milk, 3 quarts.

Breakfast at Half-past Eight o'clock, Dinner at Half-past One o'clock, Supper at Six o'clock.

DIETARY FOR NURSES AND SERVANTS.

Tea,	. . .	¼ lb. per week.
Sugar,	. . .	1 lb. „
Bread,	. . .	3 loaves (2 lb. loaves).
Butter,	. . .	½ lb.
Potatoes,	. . .	1 lb. daily.
Vegetables,	. .	3 times per week.
Meat,	. . .	½ lb. of meat or bacon daily, without bone.
Milk,	. . .	1 pint each daily.
Eggs,	. . .	1 on Friday for dinner.
Butter,	. . .	1 oz. „

ST. MARK'S OPHTHALMIC AND AURAL HOSPITAL.

Breakfast.	Dinner.	Supper.	Extra allowed (if specially prescribed).
Bread, 8 oz. Tea, 1 pint. Egg, 1.	On Tuesday and Wednesday— Roast mutton, 4 oz.; turnips or cabbage, 3 oz.; bread, 4 oz.; potatoes, 16 oz. On Monday and Saturday— Roast beef or stewed beef occasionally with 1 pint soup, 6 oz.; turnips or cabbage, 3 oz.; bread, 4 oz.; potatoes, 16 oz. On Thursday—Roast mutton, 4 oz.; turnips or cabbage, 3 oz.; bread, 4 oz.; potatoes, 16 oz. On Thursday—Roast beef, 3 oz.; turnips, 3 oz.; bread, 4 oz. or potatoes, 16 oz. On Friday—Fish, 4 oz., or eggs, 2; bread, 4 oz., or potatoes, 16 oz.	Bread, buttered, 4 oz. Tea, 1 pint, or as ordered by Dr. or Paying Patients. New milk, 1 pint.	One additional egg. Beef tea, 1 pint. New milk, 1 pint. Arrowroot, 1 pint. Rice Milk, 1 pint. Wine, or other stimulants, at discretion of medical attendant.

All patients (except those confined to bed) dine together in the Dining Hall.
Breakfast at 8 o'clock, A.M.; dinner at 1.30 o'clock, P.M.; supper at 6.30 o'clock, P.M.

FORMULARIES

Tea (6 pints.)	Beef with Broth (32 pints).	Beef Tea (8 pints).
Tea, . . . 3 oz. Sugar, . . 6 oz. New Milk, . 1 pint.	Ox Head, . . . 1 Beef, (allowing of bone,) 3 oz. to each Patient. } 4 lb. Barley, . . . } 1 lb. *or* Split Peas, . . } 1 lb. Oatmeal, . . . 2 lb. Parsley, Thyme, } to Onions, } savour Leeks or Celery, Pepper and Salt to taste. The No 2 Ordinary Diet Beef to be cut small previous to boiling, and served in the Soup. The No. 3 Ordinary Diet Beef to be served whole.	Beef, lean, without bone, 4 lb. Pepper and Salt to taste. The Beef to be cut small, and placed in cold water for three hours previous to simmering.

Whey (8 pints)	Gruel (6 pints)	Arrowroot or Rice Milk (1 pint).
New Milk, . . 6 pints. Butter Milk, . 2 pints.	Oatmeal, . . . 12 oz. Sugar, . . . 9 oz. Ginger to flavour. Steep the meal from night before, boil for two hours. **Stirabout (1 quart).** Oatmeal, . . . 4 oz. New Milk to be mixed with each quart of } ½ pint stirabout.	Arrowroot or Rice, 1 oz. Sugar, . . . 2 oz. New Milk, . . ½ pint. **Dinner Rice.** Boiled Rice, (weight} uncooked) } 4 oz. Sugar, . . . 1 oz. New Milk, . . ½ pint.

Breakfast at Half-past Seven o'clock, A.M., Dinner at Two o'clock, P.M., Supper at Six o'clock, P.M.

ROTUNDA AUXILIARY HOSPITAL.

Diet.	Breakfast.	Dinner.	Supper.
Full Diet.	Bread, 4 oz.; Tea, 1 pint; Butter, ½ oz.; or, Bread, 4 oz.; Stirabout, 1 pint; Milk, 1 pint.	4 oz. Cooked Meat, Beef or Mutton, roasted or boiled, alternately; ½ lb. Potatoes; ½ pint Broth; or, ½ pint Broth, with Meat, Rice Pudding, and Bread, 4 oz.; or, 8 oz. White Fish instead of Broth.	Bread, 4 oz.; Tea, 1 pint; or, Bread, 4 oz., and ½ pint of Gruel; or, ½ pint Stirabout and ½ pint Milk.
Low Diet.	Bread, 4 oz.; Milk, Tea, or Gruel, ½ pint Butter, ½ oz.	Bread, 4 oz.; Milk or Beef Tea, 1 pint.	Same as Breakfast.
Fever Diet.	Milk, Whey, Beef Tea, Chicken Broth, Stirabout, Bread, Arrowroot, Eggs, or Corn Flour, as ordered.		

MATERNITY HOSPITAL.

Low Diet.—2 pints hot Milk, 1 pint Gruel, 1 pint Broth. Tea, Bread, a sufficiency; Beef Tea, Eggs, or other extras when ordered.

Full Diet.—4 oz. meat in place of Broth.

For Beef Tea we allow 2 lb. beef to 5 pint water. For Broth—Stock with barley, oatmeal, leeks, &c. For Gruel—To 7 pints Milk, 1 lb. Oatmeal, 4 oz. Sugar, and a little Ginger. Tea, 3 oz. for 6 patients.

Each patient on admission shall be placed on low Diet, until the proper Diet is ordered, or by the Physicians. No extras shall be given, unless on the order of the Master or Assistant, and re-ordered unless the order thereafter is initialed on the Diet Sheet by the Physician at his

ROYAL HOSPITAL FOR INCURABLES, DONNYBROOK.

DIETARY (FULL).

Monday,. . | lb. Potatoes, 3½ oz. Tea, ½ lb. Sugar, 6 oz. Bacon, Cabbage, 1 lb. Bread, ½ pint Milk.

Tuesday,. . ½ lb. Potatoes, 6 oz. Butter, 8 oz. Mutton, 1 lb. Bread, ½ pint Milk.

Wednesday,. . ½ lb. Potatoes, ½ lb. Beef, 1 lb. Bread, ½ pint Milk.

Thursday,. . | lb. Potatoes, 6 oz. Bacon, Cabbage, 1 lb. Bread, ½ pint Milk.

Friday,. . | lb. Potatoes, Fish, 6 oz. Butter, 1 lb. Bread, ½ pint Milk.

Saturday,. . | lb. Potatoes, ½ lb. Beef, 1 lb. Bread, ½ pint Milk, 1 pint Soup.

Sunday,. . | lb. Potatoes, 6 oz. Mutton, 1 lb. Bread, ½ pint Milk.

DIETARY (INVALID).

Monday,. . | lb. Potatoes, 3½ oz. Tea, ½ lb. Sugar, 6 oz. Bacon, Cabbage, ½ lb. Bread, ½ pint Milk.

Tuesday,. . | lb. Potatoes, 2 Eggs for Dinner, 6 oz. Butter, ½ lb. Bread, ½ pint Milk.

Wednesday,. . ½ lb. Potatoes, 6 oz. Mutton, ½ lb. Bread, ½ pint Milk.

Thursday,. . | lb. Potatoes, 6 oz. Bacon, Cabbage, ½ lb. Bread, ½ pint Milk.

Friday,. . | lb. Potatoes, Fish, 6 oz. Butter, ½ lb. Bread, ½ pint Milk.

Saturday,. . | lb. Potatoes, 2 Eggs for Dinner, ½ lb. Bread, ½ pint Milk.

Sunday,. . | lb. Potatoes, 6 oz. Mutton, ½ lb. Bread, ½ pint Milk.

* Week's Tea and Sugar.

No. 8.

WESTMORLAND LOCK (GOVERNMENT) HOSPITAL.

BOARD OF GOVERNORS.

Appointed by His Excellency the Lord Lieutenant.

(19 & 20 Vic., cap. 110.)

Date of Appointment.	Members' Names.
1876, May 31st,	Edward Fottrell, esq., J.P. (Died.)
1879, February 9th,	Sir Philip Crampton Smyly, M.D., F.R.C.S.I.
1884, January 31st,	John R. Mallins, esq.
1884, November 30th,	Sir Francis R. Cruise, esq., M.D., F.R.C.P.I.
1884, May 30th,	Sir William Findlater, esq., D.L., J.P.
1884, June 12th,	Richard O'Shaughnessy, esq., M.L.
1888, February 21st,	Sir John E. Barry, Knt.
1889, February 21st,	Alderman Sir Robert Sexton, J.P., D.L.
1889, March 16th,	Charles Kennedy, esq., J.P.
1890, March 7th,	Lambert Hepenstal Ormsby, esq., M.D., F.R.C.S.I., J.P.
1890, June 23rd,	George Plunkett O'Farrell, esq., M.D., Q.R.C.S., Esq., J.P.
1890, December 31st,	Stewart Woodhouse, esq., M.D., F.R.C.S.
1891, July 11th,	John Groves Nasterson, esq.
1891, July 11th,	William Watson, esq., J.P.
1891, July 11th,	Colonel A. Verry Duveren, J.P.
1893, January 23rd,	Charles E. Lambkin, esq.
1893, March 18th,	Sir Christopher J. Nixon, M.D., F.R.C.P.
1894, September 11th,	Sir Charles A. Cameron, M.D., F.R.C.S.
1896, February 3rd,	Daniel J. Cunningham, Esq., M.D., D.C.L.
1897, February 5th,	Sir William Stokes, M.D., F.R.C.S.

JAMES WILSON HUGHES,
Registrar.

15th February, 1899.

ATTENDANCE of Governors at Meetings held during Year ended 31st March, 1899.

Date of Meetings 1898-99.					
Edwd. Pakmell, esq., J.P.					
Sir Philip C. Smyly, M.D.					
John N. Halton, esq., J.P.					
Sir Fras. R. Cruise, M.D.					
Sir Wm. Findlater, J.P., D.L.					
John E. Barry, esq.					
Richard O'Shaughnessy, esq., M.P.					
Sir Robert Sexton, J.P., D.L.					
Chas. Kennedy, esq., J.P.					
T. Fitzgerald Ormsby, esq., M.D., J.P.					
Sir George Fleming O'Farrell, M.D., J.P.					
Stewart Woodhouse, esq., M.D.					
John O. Blackburne, esq.					
Sir Wm. Wilson, J.P.					
GR. A. Vesey Darcott, J.P.					
Charles S. Lanishin, esq.					
Sir Chr. Nixon, M.D.					
Sir Charles A. Cameron, C.B., M.D.					
D. J. Cunningham, esq., M.D., D.C.L.					
Sir William Stokes, M.D.					
Corochias Philp, esq., J.P.					
George F. Brooke, esq., D.L., J.P.					
Total at each Meeting					

(Continued),

P. J. Tone, Registrar.

Board of Dublin Hospitals

49

HOUSE OF INDUSTRY (GOVERNMENT) HOSPITALS.
BOARD OF GOVERNORS.

Appointed by His Excellency the Lord Lieutenant.
(19 & 20 Vic., Cap. 110.)

1. The Right Hon. the Earl of Meath (Chairman).	7. Samuel Gordon, esq., M.D. (Died.)
2. John E. Mullins, esq., J.P.	8. Sir William Thomson, M.D., Ch.M., F.R.C.S.I.
3. Sir William Stokes, M.D., F.R.C.S.I.	9. Right Hon. Jas. H. Neale, P.C., LL.D.
4. Charles E. Martin, esq., J.P.	10. Right Hon. Thomas A. Dickson, P.C.
5. Sir John Banks, M.D., K.C.B., M.L.	11. James Murphy, esq.
6. Sir Percy R. Grace, Bart., D.L.	12. Cornelius Kelly, esq., J.P.

Joseph O'Carroll, esq., M.D., Ch.M., F.R.C.P.I.

A. SMITH,
Secretary and Superintendent.

RETURN showing the Attendance of each Member of the Board of Governors at the several Meetings held during the Year ended 31st March, 1899.

RETURN showing the Attendance of each Member of the Board of Governors at the several Meetings held during the Year ended 31st March, 1890—*continued.*

Appendix.
No. 5.
Governors,
House of
Industry
Hospitals.

Number.	Date of Meeting 1890.	1. The Right Hon. The Earl of Meath	2. John N. Mathew, Esq.	3. Dr. William Stoker, M.D., F.R.C.S.I.	4. Charles J.P.	5. William Brooke, A.O.G.	6. Dr. R.D. Lyons, M.P.	7. Percy M. Crose, Bart. J.P.	8. Samuel Gordon, Esq. M.D.	9. Sir Wm. Thomson, M.D., C.B., F.R.C.S.I.	10. The Right Hon. Mr. Meade, V.C.	11. The Right Hon. The A. Hickson, P.C.	12. James Murphy, Esq.	13. Cornelius Reddy, Esq.	14. M.J. O'Carroll, M.D.	Total Governors present.
20	January, 3.	—	—	—	—	—	5	—	—	—	—	—	—	1	1	4
21	" 10.	—	1	1	—	—	—	—	1	—	—	—	—	—	1	3
22	February, 3.	—	—	1	—	1	—	—	—	—	—	—	—	—	1	5
23	" 10.	—	—	—	—	1	1	—	1	—	—	—	—	1	1	4
24	March, 3.	—	—	—	—	1	—	—	1	—	—	—	1	1	1	4
25	" 10.	—	—	—	—	1	—	—	1	—	—	—	—	—	1	3
	Total,	—	—	1	3	15	7	—	12	—	3	—	14	15	80
	Average Attendance,	—	—	—	—	—	—	—	—	—	—	—	—	—	—	3¾

* Died April, 1889.
† Appointed to fill vacancy caused by death of Dr. Gordon.

DR. STEEVENS'S HOSPITAL.

BOARD OF GOVERNORS AND GUARDIANS.

Ex-Officio (all for the time being).

His Grace the Lord Primate.
His Grace the Lord Archbishop of Dublin.
The Right Hon. the Lord Chancellor.
The Right Hon. the Chancellor of the Exchequer.

The Right Hon. the Lord Chief Justice.
The Right Hon. the Lord Chief Baron.
The Very Rev. the Dean of Christ Church.
*The Very Rev. the Dean of St. Patrick's.
The Provost of Trinity College.

Elected.

The Right Hon. Lord Ardilaun, D.L.
*Sir Ralph S. Cusack, D.L. J.P.
Samuel G. Wilson, M.D., F.R.C.S.I.
Sir Percy Grace, Bart., D.L. J.P.
*Thomas W. Grimshaw, M.D., F.R.C.S.I., &c., Registrar-General.
*Edward Hamilton, M.D., F.R.C.S.I.

*Henry G. Tweedy, M.D., F.R.C.P.I.
*Francis B. Ormsby, M.D., J.P.
William Hockford, J.P.
*William Miller.
*Joshua J. Pim, J.P.
*William F. Geoghegan.

* Members of Standing Committee.

RETURN of Attendances of Members of Standing Committee of Governors for Year ended 31st March, 1890.

Appendix
No. 5.
Committee,
Meath
Hospital.

List of the STANDING COMMITTEE of the MEATH HOSPITAL, and the
Number of Attendances of each Member at the Board Meetings
during the Year ended 31st March, 1899.

No.	Names.	No. of Attendances	No.	Names.	No. of Attendances
1	The Earl of Meath, K.P.	—	12	John William Moore, esq., M.D., F.R.C.P.I.	73
2	The Viscount Powerscourt, K.P.	—	13	L. Heppenstal Ormsby, esq., F.R.C.S., J.P.	31
3	Arthur Andrews, esq., J.P.	13	14	George Perry, esq., J.P.	13
4	George F. Brooke, esq., D.L.	—	15	Sir William H. Porter, Bart.	1
5	Vere Ward Brown, esq., J.P.	33	16	Alderman Thomas Pile	1
6	John V. Cassidy, esq., J.P.	0*	20	Sir Philip C. Smyly, F.R.C.S., Surgeon to the Queen.	16
7	James Craig, esq., M.D.	22			
8	Wellington Darley, esq.	8			
9	Col. Sir Gerald Dease, J.P.	—	21	Sir William Stokes, F.R.C.S., Surgeon to the Queen.	13
10	Sir Percy R. Grace, Bart.	21			
11	Sir Howard Grubb, F.R.S.	3		Number of Board meetings, 24.	397
12	Sir Reginald Guinness, D.L.	13			
13	John Mitchell, esq., M.A., D.L.	9			
14	George N. Jacob, esq.	14		Average attendance at each meeting	8·67

* Died in August, 1898.

Committee
Cork-street
Fever
Hospital.

MANAGING COMMITTEE of CORK-STREET FEVER HOSPITAL, and
Number of Attendances.

No.	Names	No. of Attendances	No.	Names	No. of Attendances
1	*Abraham Shackleton,	11	11	*J. D. Fisher,	34
2	*George Drury,	35	12	William B. Wigham,	5
3	*Thomas P. Boyd,	—	13	Samuel E. Geoghegan, C.B.	—
4	*Nicholas Lynch,	76	14	*Archibald Robinson,	36
5	*Edmund J. Figgis,	—	15	Arthur Perry,	31
6	*John Wardell,	—	16	John Hendrick (Corporation Representative).	
7	*William Perrin,	7			
8	Michael Kernan,	—		No. of Meetings,	40
9	*Marcus Goodbody, J.P.	34		„ Special Meetings,	—
10	*J. J. Digges La Touche,	11		No. Quorum,	3

* Trustees.

List of GOVERNORS and their ATTENDANCE at BOARDS, at the ROTUNDA LYING-IN HOSPITAL, DUBLIN, for the Year ended 31st March, 1899.

Appendix.
No. 2.
Attendance.
Rotunda
Lying-in
Hospital.

GOVERNORS AND GUARDIANS.

President:
HIS EXCELLENCY THE LORD LIEUTENANT.

No.	Names.	Attendance.		No.	Names.	Attendance.	
		Board.	House Com.			Board.	House Com.
	Vice-Presidents:			78	James Little, Esq., M.D.		
1	Right Hon. the Lord Chancellor,			79	W. Goulding, Esq., J.P.		
2	His Grace the Archbishop of Dublin,			80	Thomas Drew, Esq., M.A.	1	—
3	Samuel F. Adair, Esq., J.P.			41	Sir Percy K. Grattan, Bart. M.D.		
4	Lord Ardilaun,			42	Robert E. Berven, Esq.	6	—
5	Sir Ralph B. Cusack,			43	R. H. Chatterton, Esq.		
6	Right Hon. the Vice-Chancellor,			44	Sir William Watson, J.P.	1	—
				45	H. T. Mons, Esq., J.P.	3	—
7	His Grace the Lord Primate,			46	George Y. Hart, Esq. LL.D.		
8	Right Hon. the Lord Mayor,			47	Sir William Sinclair, D.L.	5	—
9	Commander of the Forces,			48	O. B. Thompson, Esq.	1	—
10	Very Rev. the Dean of St. Patrick's,			49	James Murphy, Esq.	1	—
11	Ven. the Archdeacon of Dublin,	1		40	Henry Dudgeon, Esq.	5	—
12	The High Sheriff of Dublin,			41	William J. Smyly, Esq., M.D.	5	—
13	The Recorder of Dublin,	5		42	E. D. Purefoy, Esq., M.D. (Master),	12	—
14	William Fook, Esq., J.P.			43	Charles S. Martin, Esq. J.P.		
15	Thomas J. White, Esq.			44	John H. Orpen, Esq.	6	—
16	Chaworth J. Ferguson, Esq., J.P.			45	William J. Gonkling, Esq., R.C.		
17	Robert W. Shackleton, Esq., Q.C., J.P.			46	Wellington Harley, Esq.		
18	John Maunsell, Esq., J.P.			47	Alexander Knox M'Exdire, Esq.	3	—
19	Henry Watson, Esq., J.P.			48	Andrew Jameson, Esq.		
20	Charles Uniacke Townshend, Esq., J.P.			49	Arthur H. Courtenay, Esq., J.P.		
21	Robert O'Brien Furlong, Esq.	7		50	Joseph Hone, Esq.		
22	Richd. Owen Armstrong, Esq., J.P.			51	John Gordon, Esq., Q.C.	5	—
23	Charles G. Stannell, Esq.			52	H. Pomeroy Truell, Esq., M.D., D.L.	7	—
24	Anthony Traill, Esq., J.P. F.R.C.S.			53	Sir Henry Cochrane, M.D.		
25	John Jameson, Esq., J.P.			54	Hon. Judge Overend,	3	—
26	Richard G. Elkington, Esq.	11		55	W. Burroughs Stanley, Esq.		
27	Jonathan Hogg, Esq., D.L.			56	Maurice G. Knight, Esq.	2	—
				57	T. U. Pilkington, Esq.	3	—
				58	Garrett W. Walker, Esq.	2	—
				59	E. L. Tottenham, Esq.		—

Master of the Hospital.—E. Dancer Purefoy, M.D., elected November 5th, 1898.
Consulting Physician.—James Little, M.D., F.K.Q.C.P.
Consulting Surgeon.—Sir Philip Crampton Smyly, M.D., F.R.C.S.I., Surgeon-in-Ordinary to Her Majesty the Queen in Ireland.
Assistant Physicians.—Henry Wilson, L.R.C.S.I., L. & L.K.H.C.P.I., U.P., ROTUNDA HOSPITAL. Henry Jellett, M.A., M.D., L.M. ROTUNDA HOSPITAL.
Lady Superintendent.—Miss Lucy Ramsden.
Chaplain.—Rev. J. O. Gage Dougherty, M.A.
Treasurer.—The Bank of Ireland.
Secretary and Registrar.—Wyndham Cole Fitzgerald.

ROYAL VICTORIA EYE AND EAR HOSPITAL COUNCIL.

Name.	No. of Attendances.	Name.	No. of Attendances.
President—Right Hon. Viscount Monck,	4	James F. Lombard,	11
The Lord Mayor,	—	John R. Mallins,	—
Right Hon. Judge Andrews,	5	* Wm. R. J. Molloy, J.P.,	1
Augustine F. Baker,	2	John Mooney,	1
Arthur H. Benson, F.R.C.S.,	11	Mark Ferris, Jr.,	1
Hamilton Drummond, M.P.,	7	Joseph H Plui,	1
Rev. Dr. Fuller,	5	Sir Robert Sexton,	5
Sir Percy Grace, Bart.,	7	John R. Story, F.R.C.S.,	5
James Kernan, & Co.,	—	Henry R. Swanzy, F.R.C.S.,	13
Philip Little (Corporation Representative),	3	Joseph Woodlock,	5

* N.B.—Mr. Molloy was only elected to the Council in February, 1888.

Messrs. Baker, Lombard, Mooney, Ferris, Sexton, Story, and Swanzy are also members of Committees of the Council, and meet on other occasions than the Council meetings reported above.

ROYAL HOSPITAL FOR INCURABLES.

Attendances of Committee.

Name.	Meetings Attended.	Name.	Meetings Attended.
Richard Carey, esq.,	8	William Fry, jun., esq., J.P.,	12
David Drummond, esq.,	1	John Gilmore, esq.,	4
T. A. Farrell, (the late),	6	Rev. Thomas Good, D.D.	17
E. J. Figgis, esq.,	15	William Ferrin, esq.,	3
William Watson, esq.,	6	Rev. Maurice Day, M.A.	1
William Fry, esq. (Chairman),	16	M. Dillon, esq.,	2
Fane Vernon, esq., J.P. (Vice-Chairman),	15	H. Corcoran, esq.,	6
Hugh Galbraith, esq. (Hon. Treasurer),	13	Jonathan Hogg, esq., D.L.	
Orlando Bentex, esq.,	7	Very Rev. Canon Harris, D.D.	8
Orlando P. Baxter, esq., M.D.	6	His Honor Judge Kane,	6
Robert Booth, esq., J.P.	11	T. A. Kelly, esq.,	13
Henry Bewen, esq., J.P., T.C.	10	Charles Kennedy, esq.,	10
Vere Ward Brown, esq., J.P.	16	T. Pakenham Law, esq., Q.C.	4
Dr. Browne,	5	Samuel M'Comas, esq., J.P.	11
J. Rawson Carroll, esq., F.R.I.B.A.	11	James Mahony, esq.,	12
George W. Casson, esq., J.P.	5	John Mooney, esq.,	13
Abraham T. Chatterton, esq.,	9	Marcus Tertius Moses, esq., J.P.	8
Dr. Cranny,	16	Rev. Canon Religan, D.D.	9
Hamilton Drummond, esq.,	5	Robert O'Reilly, esq.,	4
Graves S. Eves, esq.,	10	John Parker, esq.,	13
Sir Wm. H. Findlater, D.L.	7	Jas. Talbot Power, esq., D.L.	7
Thomas Fitzgerald, esq.,	6	J. Hamilton Reid, esq.,	—
Edward Fottrell, (the late),	4	Thos. S. Slibharpe, (the late),	8
		O. U. Townshend, esq.,	3
		Charles K. Trouton, esq.,	14
		Graves K. Searight, esq.,	3
		John Lentaigne, esq., F.R.C.S.	7

DUBLIN CASTLE,

12th June, 1899.

SIR,

I have to acknowledge the receipt of your letter of the 11th instant, forwarding, for submission to His Excellency the Lord Lieutenant, the Forty-first Report of the Board of Superintendence of Dublin Hospitals, with Appendices.

I am, Sir,

Your obedient Servant,

D. HARREL.

The Secretary,
  Board of Superintendence of
    The Dublin Hospitals,
      85, Dawson-street.

DUBLIN: Printed for Her Majesty's Stationery Office,
By ALEX. THOM & Co. (Limited), 87, 88, & 89, Abbey-street,
The Queen's Printing Office.